MEDITATION

The Secret To Your Invisible Supply

MASTER PROPHET E. BERNARD JORDAN

FOGHORN
PUBLISHERS
"Of Making Many Books There Is No End..."

Meditation: The Secret To Your Invisible Supply

Meditation: The Secret To Your Invisible Supply
Zoe Ministries
310 Riverside Drive
New York, NY 10025
212-316-2177
212-316-5769 fax

ISBN-10: 1-934466-08-5
ISBN-13: 978-1-934466-08-7
Printed in the United States of America
©2008 by E. Bernard Jordan.
All Rights Reserved.

Foghorn Publishers
P.O. Box 8286
Manchester, CT 06040-0286
860-216-5622
860-568-4821 fax
foghornpublisher@aol.com

Prophetic Partners

Mascareen Cohen

Robin Morgan-Matthews

James Pardue

Padarrah and Wanda Moss

Mark Hicks

Perri Jones

Ralph Boyce

Gloria Taylor-Boyce

Dennis Green

Laura Higdon

Calvin Brown

Rodney B. Brooks

Basil Gibbs

Anthony Reid

Julia Fortune

Marchell Coleman

Table of Contents

Introduction

Christianity possesses some of the greatest spiritual gems not yet discovered by many of its followers. Perhaps that is why the spiritual experience is more properly referred to as a journey, rather than a destination. On a journey, particularly a long one, you may find many things along the way that may have been hidden from your eyesight, if you failed to slow down and take time to notice the scenery. For example, you may drive to work everyday, taking the same route. You may even take for granted the many different things along way that you pass by everyday, but yet did not even notice was there.

You saw it, but did not fully recognize it. Have you ever passed by a building or an old house, or even a store in your area, and simply wondered, "What does it look like inside of there?" Surely, I have wondered about many places that I have driven past. The truth is that I will only know the value of what's inside when I take the time to slow down and search within. The gems of Christianity will not just throw themselves at you in a forceful way. You must carefully search for them, and once you discover one such gem, it then becomes your responsibility to sell your lot and purchase the entire field of gems.

Again, the kingdom of heaven is like unto treasure hid in a field; the which when a man hath found, he hideth, and for joy thereof goeth and selleth all that he hath, and buyeth that field. Matthew 13:44

One such gem, which I believe may perhaps be the most precious of them all, is meditation. Of course when I mention the word meditation, especially in Christian circles, I get all kinds of different responses, mainly because of people's underexposure to the topic. Many people believe that meditation is not a Christian experience and have bequeathed the usefulness of this practice to Eastern religions: Buddhism, Transcendental Meditation, and other similar traditions. While it may appear that disciples of Eastern philosophy may lead in this area of meditation, this experience is not reserved for them alone. Meditation is for everybody, the entire world!

Meditation is the chief way to be successful in every area of your life. According to David in the very first Psalm, prosperity in life can be directly associated with one's ability to consistently meditate upon God's law day and night. If that is true then why aren't far more people in life successful? The reason is this; only the individual who understands why meditation is essential and also knows how to practice it can experience meditation in its fullest capacity. That which is practiced must be practical. One of the main hindrances with many Christian disciplines is that they are not practical.

Take for example, fasting. Fasting is a discipline that must be demonstrated before the people to show them how to properly practice fasting in order to get the full benefit from it. Some people try to fast without having a model, and at times can cause harm to their body. By following the example of those who have successfully fasted, you can receive all of the spiritual, mental, health, and ethereal benefits which all comes through fasting. The same concept can be used with regard to meditation. Meditation is more than just becoming silent. Silence has its purpose in life. However, silence alone does not produce riches. It may produce serenity and calm, but unless you focus on a desire, you will only gain a euphoric state of tranquility, lasting for a fleeting moment.

This book provides far more than that. This work will show you how meditation is intertwined all throughout the Bible, and is the common denominator for the successful in scripture. The Bible has much to say about this mystery of meditation. Here are just a few meditation scriptures of many that I love to read that display God's encouragement to all believers to make meditation a daily lifestyle.

Give ear to my words, O LORD, consider my meditation. Hearken unto the voice of my cry, my King, and my God: for unto thee will I pray. My voice shalt thou hear in the morning, O LORD; in the morning will I direct my prayer unto thee, and will look up. Psalms 5:1–3

O how love I thy law! it is my meditation all the day. Ps 119:97

My mouth shall speak of wisdom; and the meditation of my heart shall be of understanding. Psalms 49:3

It is rather difficult to speak of meditation without mentioning the use of imagination. Imagination and meditation could be considered the power twins inasmuch as one is an inverse of the other. Every great leader uses his or her imagination in order to create matter out of a realm that is void of form. Imagination gives the blueprint and meditation gives it form. Out of meditation great imaginations of the mind are born. And the progeny of those imaginations always bear forth fruit.

One thing that nearly all mystics of old share in common and hold in high regard is the daily practice of spiritual meditation. Jesus meditated. Abraham, Isaac, and Jacob mediated. Prophet Mohammad meditated. Job meditated. You too should follow the great tradition of the ancients and become one who meditates as well. A major secret revealed here is that what many Christians have thought prayer to be is really not prayer at all, at least in its highest form. Prayer is not a monologue.

Prayer is not necessarily a person thinking of words to say out loud and then launching those verbal thoughts up in the sky, hoping that God may hear them and answer them. True prayer is meditation and the key to manifestation comes through meditation. Unanswered prayer may be directly connected to improper prayer patterns. Because of your tradition, you may have believed that prayer is all about being heard, and that you receive merit by making the greatest noise unto the Lord. Surprisingly, just the opposite is true.

God favors silence and moves in that silence. But exactly what should you do while waiting in silence? And what will be gained while waiting in the silence? Those questions and so many more will be answered for you as you continue to read on. But for now, let's begin our journey into God's living quarters by making this Biblical confession with me.

Let the words of my mouth, and the meditation of my heart, be acceptable in thy sight, O LORD, my strength, and my redeemer. Psalms 19:14

—Bishop E. Bernard Jordan

CHAPTER 1

The Secret Power of Meditation

This book of the law shall not depart out of thy mouth; but thou shalt meditate therein day and night, that thou mayest observe to do according to all that is written therein: for then thou shalt make thy way prosperous, and then thou shalt have good success. Joshua 1:8

These were the very first words that Joshua spoke as a direct command to the children of Israel after they had been freed from corporeal bondage. Joshua knew intuitively that although these people had been freed in a physical sense, that they would need greater and continual assistance with regard to getting their minds free from the experience of slavery that caused them to forget who they were. Meditation was the key ingredient that would help usher them from a common existence to an extraordinary life.

For forty years the children of Israel had lived in the wilderness, receiving manna from heaven every day. Now they were going from being slaves to being free individuals, which would require a total mind shift. The manna from heaven was about to cease and if they were going to eat another day, they would have to learn essential keys that would give them perpetual access to everything they would ever need. Here Joshua delineated a universal law that when emulated, will cause you to become prosperous within the framework of your own imagination.

Some people have said, "I received a blessing beyond my wildest dreams." That sounds really spiritual but in all actuality that phrase is really a misnomer. No one is blessed or prospered beyond their wildest imagination. You can only be blessed to the extent that your imaginative mind allows you access. In short, "What you think on will determine what you receive in life."

This passage in Joshua may perhaps be one of the greatest and most user-friendly passages of scriptures in the entire Bible. Joshua clearly shows just how vitally important meditation is. *This book of the law shall not depart out of thy mouth* can be also stated as, "This book of the laws has to stay upon your lips. It has to stay in your mouth!" If the Word of God is going to truly work in your life, then you have to make the quality decision to always meditate on the Word day and night.

••• MEDITATIVE THOUGHT •••

What you think on will determine what you receive in life.

One of the most unfortunate things has happened within Christianity at large, especially in the Western world. Many believers have developed an aversion towards the practice of meditation because of their personal prejudices against other religions that freely practice and promote meditation in their daily spiritual discipline. What most Christians fail to realize is that meditation is not only for people who practice Eastern philosophy, the mystics, gurus, Buddhists, and Hindus.

Meditation is very much a Biblical practice. God is the One who prescribed this practice, and designated it as an important science that every believer should wholeheartedly embrace, particularly if one desires to receive whole life prosperity. Very often when the word science is mentioned, many Christians tend to squirm and feel quite uncomfortable, as oppressive religious dogma has so trained them to behave that way. Science merely implies that there is a system and a study.

Political science is the system of study through which one discovers how the political system works, or how to work the political system. The study of medicine is a system, an organized way to study how medicine works, and conversely how to work medicine for the benefit of humanity. With regards to natural and earth sciences, many people agree that there must be a systematic study in place in order for a person to get the maximum benefit of that subject.

It is no different with spiritual things. You must have a system of study, a science in place to delve into the mysteries of meditation in order to benefit optimally from it. God intended for His children to become masters of meditation. God makes it rather clear that the only way to enjoy sustained success in life is through meditation. Unfortunately, many leaders teach that meditation is unimportant.

••• MEDITATIVE THOUGHT •••

God intended for His children to become masters of meditation.

Many people are afraid to use the word meditation because the church has created many scarecrows. They've placed those scarecrows in the field to scare the crows away, keeping them from eating the grain. I'm afraid that the church structure, prone to the fallacies of men, purposely strategizes to keep certain life-keys in the Word of God as hidden mysteries. These leaders have convinced you that the mysteries are not intended for the average believer. They created the scarecrow. Sadly, you paid more attention to the scarecrows than to the grain that is in the field that Father has intended for you to eat and enjoy.

THE SECRET REVEALED

Thou shalt meditate therein day and night, that thou mayest observe to do.

Meditation will empower you to see and do. You cannot settle for only being a hearer of the Word, but you must be a doer of what you see being illustrated in the Word. Meditation produces an image of the Word of God in a practical sense that when followed, will lead you into prosperity. In order for faith to work in your life, you must have corresponding actions. Action is everything! What you believe must be acted upon in order for you to ever see tangible results. You may ask, "How can I meditate on that which I cannot see?" It is when you meditate that God gives you an *image* to act upon.

••• MEDITATIVE THOUGHT •••

Meditation empowers you to see and do.

Your faith will either rise to the occasion and produce the actions necessary to get the job done, or you will cower down at the very thought of moving forward in faith. You'll inevitably do one or the other. When you visualize the image that you received in meditation and then begin to exert energy in the direction of that thought, you will become a benefactor of the thought. You will be able to receive all of the desires connected with your meditative thoughts. That is how it works.

The opposite of that is when you do not take action and give substance to the images that you receive. When you fail to take corresponding actions usually it is because you are acting out of fear and confusion, leading you to begin making meaningless excuses and playing the blame game. So many people love this game and have great fun playing it daily. There are usually only two players in this game, the so-called devil and you.

So many people have such a time, using the devil as their scapegoat, their reason why they cannot produce the things that God has sovereignly placed on the inside of them. You will permanently evade all responsibility in life by continuing to blame the devil. Escaping responsibility makes some people feel good since they believe that they are off the hook. But the truth is that blaming the devil really hurts no one but you, since by doing so, you are no closer to actualizing your dreams.

More than that, there really is no devil at all. The devil is only a figment of your imagination. He or she is what you thought up in your mind and began to meditate on so much that it became a living reality to you. That is why you experience defeat, because in your mind you created defeat. Your cycle of defeat will not change until you change. Your prosperity and good success are totally dependent on your meditations.

DREAMS AND MEDITATION

What you think of on a conscious level continues to ruminate in your subconscious while you are sleeping. Sleep is the brother of death, but sleep is also another method of calling you out of the world. Sleep calls you away from the realm of materialism and worldliness and pulls you into yourself. Your dreams reveal your inner fears and expose the thieves that lurk within your temple.

God uses your sleep time to teach you the way that you should go. He has used this method since the beginning of time. Do you remember when the angel of the Lord intervened in Joseph's dream to bring him life-saving instructions? The message of the angel told him not to be afraid. Then the angel gave him instruction on exactly where he should flee to, so that he would escape the wrath of King Herod.

••• MEDITATIVE THOUGHT •••

*Your dreams reveal your inner fears
and expose the thieves that lurk
within your temple.*

*But while he thought on these things, behold, the
angel of the Lord appeared unto him in a dream,
saying, Joseph, thou son of David, fear not to take
unto thee Mary thy wife: for that which is conceived
in her is of the Holy Ghost. Matthew 1:20*

*And when they were departed, behold, the angel of
the Lord appeareth to Joseph in a dream, saying,
Arise, and take the young child and his mother,
and flee into Egypt, and be thou there until I
bring thee word: for Herod will seek the young
child to destroy him. Matthew 2:13*

Your dreams are a picture of what meditation
should look like. Under most circumstances,
when you dream you sleep through the night and

your dream is not interrupted until you awaken. That is the same way that meditation should work. When you meditate you should focus on the Word of God to you, so intently that nothing can interrupt the process.

Meditation that produces results is the kind of meditation that cannot be easily broken. You think about it, day and night. True meditation is marked by the fact that you cannot shake the thoughts associated with your meditation no matter how hard you try. Transfiguration and transformation takes place only by meditating on the Word of God. What you behold will hold you. And you will become whatever you behold.

••• MEDITATIVE THOUGHT •••

When you meditate you should focus on the Word of God to you, so intently that nothing can interrupt the process.

Nevertheless when it shall turn to the Lord, the vail shall be taken away. 2 Corinthians 3:16

The thing that begins to eclipse your vision or block your focus is taken away only when you start to turn towards the Lord. Paul continues in, 2 Corinthians 3:17 *"Now the Lord is that Spirit: and where the Spirit of the Lord is, there is liberty."* You will only find liberty where the Spirit of the Lord resides.

THE DIVINE REFLECTION

But we all, with open face beholding as in a glass the glory of the Lord, are changed into the same image from glory to glory, even as by the Spirit of the Lord. 2 Corinthians 3:18

Beholding means "to see, to mirror, to show in a mirror, to make, to reflect, and to look at oneself in a mirror." Whatever you continue to look at is the process of mirroring yourself. If you look at defeat all day, that is what you will experience in life—daily defeat. You wonder why you are being defeated and failing at everything you set out to do. It is simply because you mediate on those things all of the time. And your outcome will not change until your focus changes. Who you fly with will determine the outcome of your situation. Whatever you behold, you become. That's why I intentionally stay in the company of high achievers, since I am no more than the reflection of the company that I keep. One of the main reasons why so many people are trapped is that they refuse to let go of some of their friends. If your friends do not know who they are, in time you will not know who you are either.

You made the bad choice of telling them that they were going to be friends for life. What you didn't realize is that they were not concerned about growing and moving forward in life. They are happy making $15,000.00 a year. They have a "piece of car" that they push down the block, proudly singing the song, "We don't need no money, I've got Jesus and that's enough." The reality is that if you really have Jesus, that can most easily be recognized by having an over-abundance of supply, not just material supply but also the immaterial ethereal supply, which yields tangible substance.

Understand that in God there is no lack. There is no shortage. So you can continue to make excuses and continue to blame this one and that one, but nothing will change in life until you do. A friend of mine says that whenever he wants to lose weight, he lays pictures of thin people all over his house. He continues to behold them until he loses weight. The principle really works! You have to meditate on the images of what you want to become and then those images will become your divine reflection.

Before I purchased my first house, I had to start gazing at house magazines. After that I got mad with my situation in order to initiate developmental changes. I went out and purchased a bunch of books and magazines showcasing five and six million dollar houses. Seeing other people live at that level of wealth provoked something in me. I never got mad at them for living on that level. In fact, I would bless them instead. Reality was that nothing changed for me until I got mad with my present condition. But change won't happen until you get an image of something new. Don't get mad with others, get mad at yourself.

Rosa Parks had to get angry about sitting at the back of the bus, before her inward protest declared her right to sit in the front. Are you angry about something? If you are, your mind is signaling and demanding for a change! Nothing changes in your life until you get so mad about the thing that has to change that you demand inwardly that a change will happen. When you do that, you will begin to imagine a totally different world, one that reflects the express image of how you desire things to be, from your inward perspective. So let's review some major areas that you have learned so far.

1. Always qualify those who walk with you.
2. Whatever you behold you become.
3. You cannot change your future until you get mad at your present.

TRUTH VERSUS FACTS

All of us are in a state of metamorphosis, metaphorically speaking, transitioning from a larva to a beautiful butterfly. Transformation beckons unto every soul. People tend to be overly concerned about the facts. But the facts are not necessarily truth. What you should be most concerned about is what God's Word says about you.

It is a fact that Rahab the harlot should have went to hell after she told a lie concerning the spies she was hiding. Instead God declared her act as one of righteousness, rewarding her with the highest honor of being part of the direct lineage of Jesus. It was a fact that David killed Goliath, and one of the Ten Commandments is "Thou Shalt Not Kill." But the truth is that David's purpose and destiny ushered him into an eternal glory. The facts did not hold him back. You may be confronted by facts that limit your ability to become more, to achieve greatness in life, and to live life as a contributor rather than a taker. To move past those limiting beliefs you must lock into your purpose by echoing the voice of God concerning you. You will only be able to hear God's voice clearly when you have meditated long enough in His presence to discern His plan for you.

The Father is completely blind to the facts. And more importantly, the truth in God's eyes is never what you are right now but only that which you will become. It was a fact that Jacob was not Esau, but rather an impersonator. Despite that fact, Jacob received the blessing that was originally designated for his brother. How is that? Jacob understood even in the most conniving way, how meditating on the desire would yield him that desire. He understood how feeling brings your desires closer to your actual experience. What you feel like becomes the kind of blessing you receive.

And Isaac said unto Jacob, Come near, I pray thee, that I may feel thee, my son, whether thou be my very son Esau or not. Genesis 27:21

Looking at the facts is not often a positive experience because looking at the facts produces bondage, not freedom. It may be a fact that you have been divorced more than once. The facts suggest that because of marital failure you should not be involved with ministry any longer. The facts may imply that your life is not model-worthy and that you are no longer capable of leading people spiritually because of your failure. If you persist in focusing on those facts, then that will become your meditation.

••• MEDITATIVE THOUGHT •••

You will only be able to hear God's voice clearly when you have meditated long enough in His presence to discern His plan for you.

You should rather meditate on God's original plan for your life, the one that He is committed to helping you to fulfill. The truth is that you must remain in ministry, and that you may very well be far more capable to help people in similar life challenging situations. Understand and accept the truth that your life is not based on any facts. Your life is based on how you feel. The key to meditation is the mountain upon which transformation takes place. Here is the contemplative sound, "If you change your thinking, you can change your outcome."

••• MEDITATIVE THOUGHT •••

*Your feelings determine the type
of blessing you receive.*

And be not conformed to this world: but be ye transformed by the renewing of your mind, that ye may prove what is that good, and acceptable, and perfect, will of God. Romans 12:2

Be not conformed to the present arrangement of this in the world. When you choose to do the accepted thing and think like the world thinks, you then lessen your spiritual capacity to meditate. Meditation requires that you totally focus on the will of the Father, not man's will for your life. Often His will is in direct contradistinction to what man believes you should be, have, and do.

For example, many people of the world collectively believe that a preacher should not drive a luxury car such as a Rolls Royce or a Bentley. If you choose to conform to their ideals for you, then you are in direct violation of God's purpose and design for your life. Be not conformed! The world dictates how you should dress, where you should live, and even what you should eat. Be not conformed!

Nearly fifteen years ago, an internationally known spiritual healer, who is a dear friend of mine, fell for the bait. He was driving a late model Mercedes Benz at the time, purchased for him by his ministry partners. The media and his critics began complaining about the car that he drove, proposing that he should drive a car more humble, and one that was not as costly as the Mercedes Benz. Trying to please them, he sold his car and then purchased a new Lincoln Town Car, which was nearly forty thousand dollars less than the Mercedes Benz car.

After going through that major transition with hopes that his critics might become clearer about his genuineness, the same crowd of accusers began to write more disparaging remarks and articles, suggesting that he get rid of the Lincoln Town car too. Where my friend missed it was in believing that he could actually please the world, or in other words, a worldly system of thought. Worldly thinking is synonymous with worldly meditations. The truth is that they would never be pleased, even if he chose to walk instead. The world does not have the spiritual capacity to comprehend what God has designed for you, since their minds aren't renewed. So stop trying to convince them otherwise.

They even regulate what you should say. Jesus did not conform, not even with His language, as there were times when Jesus used coarse words in making a statement to certain people. His behavior did not always conform to the world's image of a savior. Once, he disrupted the temple, overturned the tables, took a whip and whipped the thieves out of the House of the Lord. He called people snakes, and dogs, not conventional lingo for the messiah. Being conventional did not matter to him, as He was not trying to fit it at all. Jesus is the truth. He knew that, so that became His dominant focus. Knowing that He was the truth was Jesus' meditation.

One of the reasons why some Christian sects are so powerless is because they have spent years meditating on the wrong Jesus. They've meditated on a blond haired, blue eyed, frail framed Jesus as seen in Hollywood depictions, paintings, and lithographs. If you meditate upon the image of Jesus that Hollywood has presented, you will never know Him.

. . . *that ye may prove what is that good, and acceptable, and perfect, will of God.*

Stop searching for the will of God. The will of God is not to be found. It is not lost. The will of God is to be proven. It is an insult for you to say, "I am trying to find God's will." His will is already found; it exists eternally in the Word of God. It is your job to prove it. You ask, "How do I prove it?" Just simply be Christ. God's will and Himself are indivisible and inseparable. God's will is for you to become god.

••• MEDITATIVE THOUGHT •••

To understand meditation is to
understand what you are picturing.

And you will only become Him through meditation. To understand meditation is to understand what you are picturing. You have received the manifestation of what you pictured in life. In order to change your life, change what you picture, change the image. Focus on His reflected image in His Word, then your life will begin to transform into the express image of God. When you embrace God's Word you embrace Him. God is waiting for you to make a quality decision and perceive life with Him being manifested through you.

CHAPTER 2

The Heart That Sings In Grace

Let the word of Christ dwell in you richly in all wisdom; teaching and admonishing one another in psalms and hymns and spiritual songs, singing with grace in your hearts to the Lord. Colossians 3:16

The "Word of God" as defined in Greek is the word LOGOS, which actually means, something said. This meaning actually encompasses the thought of God. So then, the Word of God is a speech, a word uttered by a Living Voice, a conception or an idea. The Word was made flesh—conceived—and dwelt among us. Jesus is the Word of God, the very thought of God, He is God's expression. Each Word that God expresses is an expression of the thoughts that He thinks toward you. God's Word is literally the meditations of His heart.

Your wealth and prosperity begin in your thoughts. They begin in the songs that you sing and meditate on in your mind. Before you can become physically rich, your mind must be wealthy first. And the way that your mind becomes wealthy is by depositing real assets into the rich soil of your mind. Your transformation in life will only come through the renewing of your mind, not the removing of your mind. Your thoughts are the living and tangible expression of your passions and desires. The reason why your thoughts are tangible and not solely ethereal is because all thoughts are things. So you must possess a desire before a blessing manifests. Desire is the proof that your visions exist.

To appoint unto them that mourn in Zion, to give unto them beauty for ashes, the oil of joy for mourning, the garment of praise for the spirit of heaviness; that they might be called trees of righteousness, the planting of the LORD, that he might be glorified. Isaiah 61:3

```
••• MEDITATIVE THOUGHT •••

Your wealth and prosperity
begins in your thoughts.
```

So many people go through life and instead of
allowing their dreams and visions to guide them,
they walk through life allowing negative things to
pile on their plates such as fear, indecision, confusion, pain, and antipathy. All of those things crowd
one's ability to properly meditate. The ultimate
goal of your meditation is not to acquire things.
Quite honestly you can have a whole lot of things
without using meditation at all. Hard work can get
you things. Stealing can get you things. So the goal
of meditation is to usher you into a perpetual state
of praise.

```
••• MEDITATIVE THOUGHT •••

All thoughts are things.
```

Meditation ushers you into the presence of God, the place where labor ceases. That is why the victories that you will experience in that place will seem effortless. In His presence there is fullness of joy and also rest. People will wonder how you are able to do so much in such a limited amount of time. You are only capable of doing those things because you have tapped into the source by meditating on His Word day and night.

*This book of the law shall not depart out of thy mouth; but **thou shalt meditate therein day and night,** that thou mayest observe to do according to all that is written therein: for then thou shalt make thy way prosperous, and **then thou shalt have good success**. Joshua 1:8 (bold is author's own)*

In this realm of praise you will catch a glimpse of continuous victory. Things that you could never perceive with your natural eyes are ever so clear in your mind, because Spirit has the unusual ability to make the invisible become visible to you. To the onlooker who does not understand the power of meditation, they'll look at you and wonder what in the world are you praising God for. They will look at your present conditions, and where you are right now in your life financially, emotionally, and relationally and then believe that you should be in a depression rather than in a praising state of mind.

••• MEDITATIVE THOUGHT •••

Desire is the proof that your visions exist.

What they may not realize is that people who meditate on God's Word never wait to praise God after manifestation has come. They never delay their praise. You praise God in advance, knowing deep within that what you have meditated upon will come to pass. When it looks like you should be heavy in your spirit, God gives you the garment of praise in exchange for your heaviness. The ultimate goal here is that like Jesus, we must become the Word made flesh. But that transformation can only be manufactured in the minefields of your sustained thoughts.

And the Word was made flesh, and dwelt among us, (and we beheld his glory, the glory as of the only begotten of the Father,) full of grace and truth. John 1:14

You are God's motive. He intended for you to be here in His eternal thoughts. Therefore, you are not an accident or mistake. The reason why you exist is because you were a part of God's meditative thoughts, which became a physical reality. You—the motive of God—was made flesh. You are really a thought that has been actualized in the flesh. You could not be born at any other time than when you were born. God needed you to be here now. You are His Word coming to pass in the earth.

Then said I, Lo, I come (in the volume of the book it is written of me,) to do thy will, O God. Hebrews 10:7

Before you entered into this earth realm, there was a book written and sealed just for you. No one was worthy to loose the seal of your book other than the Lamb of God! Understand that you are priceless. Your thoughts, words, and meditations will change greatly when you come into the knowledge of who you actually are. Most people do not know who they are. Far more are confused about their function on this earth. As a result of that many people tend to meditate on things such as, "why I am here," and, "where am I going?"

••• MEDITATIVE THOUGHT •••

*You are God's Word coming
to pass in the earth.*

There is nothing inherently wrong with wanting to know your life's purpose. However, the longer that you are ignorant about whom you are, and the express reason you were made, you will never be like God, you will never be God. The primary function of God as stated in the very beginning is Elohim—Creator of heaven and earth. So then you too must realize your optimal self by becoming a co-creator with God. You can never do this though when your mind is preoccupied, trying to figure out what you are doing on earth.

```
••• MEDITATIVE THOUGHT •••

Your thoughts, words, and meditations will
change greatly when you come into the
knowledge of who you actually are.
```

Those concerns must be totally resolved inside of you. There should be no question at all as to who you are and why you are here. That whole matter has been predetermined from the foundation of the earth. When you really begin to grasp hold of who you are, you will come into the understanding that you were here before you were here. Really you've been here before. You preexisted with God in eternity past. Perhaps that is why things that you cannot remember seeing seem so familiar to you. That is why you experience déjà vu.

Before I formed thee in the belly I knew thee; and before thou camest forth out of the womb I sanctified thee, and I ordained thee a prophet unto the nations. Jeremiah 1:5

Before you had any form (legs, hands, a heart, lungs, and so forth), God knew you intimately. God knew who you were; He knew your name before your parents named you. More than that, God knew your real name, the one that He would call you by for the rest of your life. It is that name that has the most redemptive meaning. God changed Abrams' name to Abraham, the name under which he received the promise.

Many people are still missing out on God's promise, because God can only give the promise to the one who bears His Name and His Likeness. God's name is "I AM." God, as your supreme model, literally used the power of meditation conjoined with creation to bring you into the earth realm. He meditated on the thing that He wanted to see in creation.

When God wanted to make man, He mediated on man long enough and focused enough that man came into being. What you focus on will come into being. You have in your life everything that you have focused on, on a conscious or subconscious level. It is possible to meditate on things of which you are not aware. Whether you are aware or not, you will still be rewarded with the product of your meditative thoughts. Have you ever wondered why the youth culture in nearly ever generation is so fascinated and dominated by music?

••• MEDITATIVE THOUGHT •••

Many people are still missing out on "the promise" because God can only give the promise to the one who bears His Name and His Likeness. God's name is "I AM."

Little babies can sometimes hum the tune to the latest hit, even though they cannot even read a word or barely pronounce their name properly. Songs, hymns, and melodies do not only represent your favorite hits list. Songs, hymns, and melodies represent the continued meditations of your heart.

It symbolizes the song that won't go away. And the longer that you sing that song, the closer it becomes to you. It's like second nature. Fill in the missing lyrics to this popular song, A,B,C,D, __ __ __, H,I,J,K, __ __ __ __ __, Q,R,S, __ __ __, W,X,Y, and __.

> ••• MEDITATIVE THOUGHT •••
>
> *What you focus on will come into being.*

Did you get it right? If you did, it's only because you have so meditated on the alphabet song that it is now a part of you. You need no practice or warm up. You just know. God meditated on man so intensely that God became man, and man became God. That is why God knew Jeremiah long before he arrived here on earth. God had conversations with Jeremiah before he was born. God had a relationship with Jeremiah since the very beginning of time.

God's relationship with you did not start when you began walking with the Lord. His relationship with you began long before that. So when did you begin? Certainly not when you were born from your mother's womb. You began when God began. And since God has no beginning, neither do you. You were always in God's consciousness waiting for the perfect time in history to appear. *But when the fulness of the time was come, God sent forth his Son, made of a woman, made under the law. Galatians 4:4*

••• MEDITATIVE THOUGHT •••

You have in your life everything that you have focused on, on a conscious or subconscious level.

GOD IS THINKING OVER YOU

What does it mean for God to think over you? You may know what it means when a person thinks about you. That means that you are the central thought in their mind. The very thought of you dominates that person's mind all of the time. That is good. But what is better than God thinking about you is when God thinks over you. His thought superimposes your thoughts and His thought becomes the dominant thought in the process. God knows everything. He already knows the outcome of everything from the very beginning.

Anytime God asks a question, it is never so that He can get clarity on the subject. God only asks so that you can get clarity. He asks you questions so that you can gain a greater revelation about yourself. He already knows the answer when He asks. The problem is that you don't always know the answer, yet you should. The answer is within you. Let's explore this realm of mystery a little further. When God came to Adam in the Garden of Eden to inquire of the sin that he and Eve had committed, God asked Adam where he was.

And the LORD God called unto Adam, and said unto him, Where art thou? And he said, I heard thy voice in the garden, and I was afraid, because I was naked; and I hid myself. Genesis 3:9–10

God did not ask this question because he did not know where Adam was. God asked Adam this question because Adam did not know where he was. Adam did not know where he was in relation to God. He did not know that He was God. God wasn't lost, Adam was. That is why the serpent beguiled Eve, making her believe that she was less than God. It is this mistake, the error of believing in other Gods other than yourself, which causes you to lose your true identity.

••• MEDITATIVE THOUGHT •••

Anytime God asks a question, it is never so that He can get clarity on the subject. God only asks so that you can get clarity.

When that happens you live life in search of the thing that already exists on the inside of you. Another thing is that God usually speaks in esoteric terms, not in our common everyday vernacular. When God asked Adam, *Where art thou?* He was not talking about a place, or space within an area. God was talking about identity. God knew where Adam was both in the natural and in the supernatural. Yet His objective was to get Adam to recognize this.

. . .they heard the voice of the LORD God walking in the garden in the cool of the day: Genesis 3:8

Is it possible that words can actually walk? Absolutely! Here the Bible says that God's Words actually walked in the garden. You have a word walking behind you all of the time. It is the Word of the Lord, your prophetic word. When you receive a prophetic word and merge your word with faith it becomes a force field that goes up and around your life. Your word begins to hover all about you, and will literally follow you all the days of your life.

Have you ever heard someone testify about how God intervened in their life, displaying His Grace and healing power, after the doctor has given them a negative report of impending death? They were slated for death, yet a voice came behind them declaring just the opposite, proclaiming healing. That is God thinking over you. Since His thoughts are healing and wholeness, His thoughts prevail, particularly when you yield your thoughts to His plan. God's angels are always around you. First you must release the solitary image in your mind of the traditional thought that sees angels as winged creatures flying around in the heavens. Angels are messengers of thought.

And saith unto him, If thou be the Son of God, cast thyself down: for it is written, He shall give his angels charge concerning thee: and in their hands they shall bear thee up, lest at any time thou dash thy foot against a stone. Matthew 4:6

Look at this scripture from an esoteric viewpoint and you will discover that Jesus was really speaking about thoughts, not literal angels soaring around in paradise. God gave His thoughts charge over Jesus. God would think over His Son, and when God thought over Him the thoughts of death were supplanted by thoughts of life. When God thinks over you it is very much like how His Spirit hovered over the waters in the beginning of time.

*The earth was without form, and void; and dark-
ness was on the face of the deep. And the Spirit of
God was hovering over the face of the waters.
Genesis 1:2 NKJV*

God thinks over you, His thoughts hover
over your life so that His intentions become
formed right in your midst. Stop looking for the
winged angels and instead look for God's
thoughts. You ask, "How will I know if the
thoughts I am thinking are really God's thoughts
and not other-minded contemplations?" You will
know how to identify God's thoughts in you all
of the time when you begin to see your limiting
beliefs rendered null and void.

The decisions of the doctor to confine you to a lifestyle of drug dependency and hospice care will suddenly be rendered null and void. The decision of the financier to deny your loan or repossess your assets will be rendered null and void. The decision to terminate your marriage will be rendered null and void. God's thought over you reverses the plan of anyone who opposes your forward progress in life. His thoughts become dominant and your thoughts become submissive to God's. When you begin to really understand angelic visitation, you will discover that angels of God are simply the thoughts of God. He gives his angels charge over thee, His angel, His Word.

Be not forgetful to entertain strangers: for thereby some have entertained angels unawares.
Hebrews 13:2

When you reject strangers you may be denying God's thoughts to have access into your life and experience. So be kind to those who bring good news, angels, for they carry the thoughts of God into your life. God thinks over you. After the Holy Spirit impregnated the Virgin Mary, He overshadowed her. The angel, who was a thought, came to bring glad tidings. God wants you to know that you are a thought. You are a point of view. More than that, you are God's point of view. That alone makes you righteous in His eyes.

> ••• MEDITATIVE THOUGHT •••
>
> *God thinks over you, His thoughts hover over your life so that His intentions become formed right in your midst.*

So the thing that you behold in your mind, you visit. When you constantly run into the same problem, it is because you are gazing into the same mirror everyday. You have not changed what you are looking at. And before anything changes in your life you must change the image before your eyes.

And looking upon Jesus as he walked, he saith, Behold the Lamb of God! John 1:36

The Apostle John said, "Behold the Lamb of God." John was only able to see Jesus as the Lamb of God because that is the image that he firmly held in his imagination. As long as He imaged Jesus in his meditative thoughts he only saw Jesus. What you look at is what you become. In many cases you become even greater than what you imagine. Jesus even said in Luke 7:28 *There is not a greater prophet than John the Baptist.* John the Baptist became that which he beheld. What are you beholding? Whatever you are beholding is actually holding you. The Spirit of God is hovering over you, intending to reign over your thoughts.

CHANGE YOUR VISION

What you focus on you will become. That is a pretty sobering thought. What you listen to you will become. The African slaves used to sing Negro spirituals while they were working in the fields. The songs that they sung were songs that focused on freedom. Some of these strong hearts never experienced freedom, yet their offspring experienced it. They saw freedom for their children, and freedom came. So you must learn to change your vision and change the tune that is constantly ringing in your head. You learn by what you see.

What are you looking at? Read books about success and prosperity. Study the lives of high achievers. As you gaze upon their lives you will become the pressed out image of them. If you keep company with negative people in time you too will become negative, because they are in your prevailing vision. You have to change what you see. For what you see is what you will be compelled to meditate on. You will never come into the fulfillment of prosperity if you persist in visioning impoverished surroundings.

It doesn't matter if you live in the low-income housing projects, go out and purchase a book of mansions and stare at those houses every single day of your life. Meditate on them. After there is a change in your thinking, a change will come in your surroundings. It has to! Build yourself a dollhouse mansion if you can and place it in a part of your apartment where you are bound to see it all of the time. Maybe you should place it right at the foot of your bed so that you can see it upon lying down each night and waking up in the morning time.

> ••• MEDITATIVE THOUGHT •••
>
> *If you keep company with negative people in time you too will become negative, because they are in your prevailing vision.*

You should go to bed with the dominant thought of your inner desires on your mind. While you are asleep, your subconscious mind will absorb your daily meditations, and Spirit will figure out a way to make the thing that you desire come into full manifestation. You never have to worry about how. All you have to do is change your vision. Change your song. When you do that, your outcome will change. For what you look upon is what you will become. God is not in favor of you possessing a welfare mentality.

••• MEDITATIVE THOUGHT •••

You have to change what you see. For what you see is what you will be compelled to meditate on.

He does not want you to live in undesirable conditions, living crowded and confused. That is no way for a King's child to live. It is His will for you to be blessed and walk in supernatural abundance. Don't be fooled into ascribing to this "by and by" concept, which says you will be blessed "by and by", when we all get to heaven. Don't be fooled by the lie which says that you will only be blessed when we reach heaven. That's not true. God has your blessing reserved for you, right now. Preoccupation with the future causes you to consort with a thief that robs you of your present.

Why allow your future to rob you when your future can become a present reality if you just permit it to be so? Your vision of wealth and abundance may not be immediately revealed in the material realm. That is fine. Continue to walk in the confidence that you already have the fruit of what you see. Become the Word made flesh and become a reflection of the will of The Father. It is God's greatest desire to make all things new unto you. That will only happen when you change your vision and begin to murmur in your mind the sound of the new song of the Lord forecasting a brand new day.

CHAPTER 3

The Art of Transformation

And be not conformed to this world: but be ye transformed by the renewing of your mind, that ye may prove what is that good, and acceptable, and perfect, will of God. Romans 12:2

There are so many people who attempt to transform their lives through external means. Some people will change their clothing, color their hair, have plastic surgery performed on them, or go on a drastic diet, all in an attempt to change their internal disarray. While none of those things are necessarily bad, those things alone cannot produce the kind of change necessary to bring about lasting results in life. Transformation must be achieved by exercising other muscles, not just your biceps and triceps.

In order to attain transformation you must regularly exercise the muscle of your mind. As with any bodily exercise, if you don't work your muscles on a regular basis, your muscles will become flaccid. The principle reason why you are not able to produce much needed changes in your life is because your mind has been weakened through lack of exercise. It has lost strength. That is because you have not exercised it with the traction of Truth.

MIND RENEWAL

How do you locate the center of your transformation? The key to your transformation can be easily found in between your two ears. If you want God to transform your life entirely, allow Him free access into the sacred soil of your mind. Allow His Word to become your primary focus. Renew your mind through meditation. The word renew literally means to make new again, to restore, or to bring into being again. Mind renewal can be compared with the experience of being born again. Every time your mind becomes renewed in an area, you are being born again into a new awareness.

If you haven't had a mind renewal in the area of healing, then you will remain sick and diseased. You won't be sick because that is your plight, but rather because you are not aware of the access that you have to healing. Your mind does not see healing as an option because it has not been renewed, thus preventing it from becoming aware of infinite possibilities concerning health and wholeness. You will make routine visits to the doctor every time you feel bad because going to the doctor is the only solution that you are aware of.

You can even go to the doctor's and continually get sent back home with misdiagnosis, feeling just a badly as you did before you went to see him or her. The next time you feel sickly, intuitively you go right back to the same doctor that could not help you the last time. Why is that? The reason you do that is because you are not aware of anything other than that. Once you become aware of higher truths, then you will become open to a level of transformation available to all, yet few seize its benefits.

••• MEDITATIVE THOUGHT •••

Every time your mind becomes renewed in an area, you are being born again into a new awareness.

If you struggle with acquiring and maintaining money, then your mind needs to be renewed in that area. Your money needs to be born again. And you must transform your mind in the area of how you think about and deal with money. Another area that you have to conquer is the church's traditional bondage teaching concerning money and its relationship with God. Many songs and hymns that are sung in churches every Sunday speak of a God who lives somewhere over the rainbows, who in His own precious time will work things out for you. That train of thought has put an unnecessary burden on God to do something different than that which He has already done.

God has already supplied your need. He has already made you wealthy. You are healed. However, none of those things will matter at all if your mind has not been renewed to that reality. You must become aware of those things in order for you to partake of its fruit. Have you ever driven by a certain building in town but you did not know what it was? It may have been a retail store, selling niche goods that you were looking for.

••• MEDITATIVE THOUGHT •••

Once you become aware of higher truths, then you will become open to new levels of transformation.

Instead of stopping to look in the store to see what was inside, you just kept on driving by. You did that for years. The goods that you could have purchased at the nearby store that you drove by every day, you end up purchasing somewhere else, about twenty or thirty miles further. You may have even purchased an inferior product. Why was that? You were not aware that the store was there, and you were unaware of what the store offered. Your mind had to become renewed, reprogrammed if you will, to the many options available to you.

Mind renewal will bring you to a place that you will be rebuilt, reconditioned, reconstructed, and restored. You are being made over again! Dare to believe this by faith! Faith is the key that will change your present and bring your future to pass. In order for God's will to manifest in your life, you have got to believe it into manifestation by an act of faith.

ARE PEOPLE SEEING GOD IN YOU?

As you begin to renew your mind through medi-tation you will begin to show forth God. People will be able to see the Christ on the inside of you beaming like a high-wattage halogen lamp. When people see you they should see the express image of the Father in you. Philip wanted to see the Father, but did not realize that everything that the Father was, was manifested in Jesus. So when Philip saw Jesus he was literally looking at the glory of the Father, but did not know it. There should be no difference when people see you from when they see God.

Philip saith unto him, Lord, shew us the Father, and it sufficeth us. Jesus saith unto him, Have I been so long time with you, and yet hast thou not known me, Philip? he that hath seen me hath seen the Father; and how sayest thou then, Shew us the Father? Believest thou not that I am in the Father, and the Father in me? the words that I speak unto you I speak not of myself: but the Father that dwelleth in me, he doeth the works. John 14:8–10

Seeing yourself as God may be a long stretch for you, particularly if you have been exposed all of your life to a religion that teaches you the primary message of the serpent, *ye shall be as gods (Genesis 3:5).* If you do not already know that you are God, then you will always settle for being as god, second best. You may at first think that such a lofty position is unattainable for you. You may think that your life is so busy, and at times it seems like it is out of control.

••• MEDITATIVE THOUGHT •••

When people see you they should see the express image of the Father in you.

How then can you possess the discipline to meditate on the Word of God and bring about the balance in your life that is so needed? Here is a word of comfort for you. Don't worry about your life appearing to be perfect as a requirement for you to receive your transformation. Believe it or not, God usually comes into your world when it is all out of sync, all confused and chaotic. Your new beginning starts at midnight. Your new day actually starts in the evening time, when it is darkest outside. It all starts for you when things are seemingly disorganized and messed up.

Get excited if your life seems like a scattered puzzle. That is a clear sign that you, your mind, and everything that pertains to you are all going to be born again. It has been said that, "Necessity is the mother of invention." Most inventions arise because there is a point of confusion, or a problem in desperate need of a solution. Right now there is something that is inside of you that is really frustrating you. More often than not, the thing that frustrates you the most is the very thing that you are called to solve.

God has called you to be a prophet to that situation, speaking and declaring the word of the Lord that will bring about transformation. But remember that before you can transform anything in your world or in the cosmos, you must first transform yourself. Transformation is no hidden thing at all. Everybody you come into contact with will know that you have been transformed. When Moses was in the presence of God, he could not hide it. When he came down from the mountain, everyone knew that he had been in the presence of God, because it was written all over his face.

And it came to pass, when Moses came down from mount Sinai with the two tables of testimony in Moses' hand, when he came down from the mount, that Moses wist not that the skin of his face shone while he talked with him. And when Aaron and all the children of Israel saw Moses, behold, the skin of his face shone; and they were afraid to come nigh him. Exodus 34:29–30

••• MEDITATIVE THOUGHT •••

Before you can transform anything in your
world or in the cosmos, you must
first transform yourself.

TURNING GOD UPSIDE DOWN

God cannot be limited or charted by time. He lives outside of time and has given humanity the gift of time as a way of measuring our progress in life. So then, for your understanding, God is called the Alpha and Omega; the beginning and the end. He is, in truth, endless—from eternity past to eternity future. But for the sake of our illustration we understand that the beginning and the end, and everything in between, are ALL GOD. God has always existed. Only God has original thoughts since He is the originator of all things. Anything that is "other than" God can only take what God has said and try to turn it upside down.

That is what we call subverting the truth. There is but one power and that is the power of God. Witchcraft derives from this same source; it has the same power. Witchcraft is merely God turned upside down, which is tantamount to the abuse of prayer. Witches do pretty much the same things that Bible believing, Holy Spirit filled Christians do, except that they do it turned upside down. Their voodoo doll is intercession turned upside down. They are standing in the gap, but instead of closing it, they widen it with schemes and manipulations.

A spiritual person once said, "Spiritual power can be likened to a car. A car, as beautiful as it is, can be a vehicle of great service if the person operating it has a valid driver's license, and a current registration. If one gets caught driving without those things in place, or if one gets in an accident without those things being renewed, then the car will become a curse rather than a blessing to the driver."

There is nothing wrong with the car, but there is a problem with the operator. That same thing goes for power. There is absolutely nothing wrong with spiritual power, but you've got to qualify those that are operating in it, making sure that they have the proper credentials to practice the presence of God. If they do not, then they are operating illegally, which is turning God upside down.

••• MEDITATIVE THOUGHT •••

There is absolutely nothing wrong with spiritual power, but you've got to qualify those that are operating in it, making sure that they have the proper credentials to practice the presence of God.

MEDITATING ON YOUR TESTIMONY

There are so many lessons that you can learn from your own life's experiences. That is why your own personal testimony is so vitally important. The things that you have endured, and came out on top in life, are predictions of how great your future is. Testimonies are a great form of meditation in that you get to rehearse your victories in life, and the process in which you've journeyed to arrive at that point.

Remembering how God brought you through your wildernesses will only serve as a reminder that you are no longer there, and that your latter days are so much more exciting than your former. Another thing that is so remarkable about your testimony is that other people can vicariously live the triumphs of your testimony by simply hearing it.

And they overcame him by the blood of the Lamb, and by the word of their testimony; and they loved not their lives unto the death. Revelation 12:11

It is rather interesting that your testimony is placed on the same equal level as the blood of the lamb. That is powerful! Christian scholars have always taught that there was nothing more sacred, nothing higher in purpose and redemptive value than the shed blood of Jesus Christ. But here we see that your testimony also has redemptive power, the same power that Jesus' blood has. Through your testimony not only will you be able to maintain the victory, but you will also allow others to experience and live your victory. The evidence of your manifested victory brings about the substance needed for your next miracle.

••• MEDITATIVE THOUGHT •••

Testimonies are a great form of meditation in that you get to rehearse your victories in life, and the process in which you've journeyed to arrive at that point.

When Jesus got ready to feed the multitudes He did not feed them with the two fish and the five loaves, but rather with what was left over, the fragments. *And they did eat, and were all filled: and there was taken up of fragments that remained to them twelve baskets. (Luke 9:17)* God has some miracles that are "left over." What are the left over miracles? Your testimony is the left over miracle. When you forget your testimony you will not have the substance to carry you through life's storms. You need to be able to say like Jesus, "Peace be still." When you declare "peace be still," you will bypass many sufferings in life, as that declaration will cause faith to rise up in your soul, even amidst the most tumultuous storm.

You can only declare "Peace Be Still" when you know, based on prior events, that God stilled other storms in your life. You speak peace based on God's Word and the word of your own testimony. The senior saints used to say; "If God did it before, surely He will do it again." That is confidence speaking aloud. It's not confidence in your own self but rather confidence in the living God. So you need to rehearse and meditate on your own miracles.

There have been times in my life when the enemy of my mind has tried to visit me with discouragement, and I had to break out into a private testimony service. I would call the prophets of my mind to prophesy my breakthrough. You too have prophets resting in your consciousness. Your mind is a prophet. You just have to discern whether it is a true prophet or a false prophet.

••• MEDITATIVE THOUGHT •••

You can only speak peace based on God's Word and the word of your own testimony.

Periodically, I have to reach back in my memory and recall when God began Zoë Ministries with only ten people. Back then we had to believe God to pay all of our bills with just ten members in our church. There were times when I did not have any clue as to how we would pay the bills at the ministry or my personal bills. I had to meditate on the scripture that let me know that I can call those things that be not as though they were. I rested on Abraham's promise. And God's promise to Abraham became my private covenant with Him.

(As it is written, I have made thee a father of many nations,) before him whom he believed,

even God, who quickeneth the dead, and calleth those things which be not as though they were. Romans 4:17

As a result of that meditation and calling forth, we have never been late. Another time I can clearly remember is when God told me to go on national television. At that time we had only one hundred and fifty members, worshipping in a hotel, the Doral Inn Hotel on Lexington Avenue, in New York. We did not have the expansive budget that many of the mega-churches had. Not only that, we had no idea at all how incredibly expensive television costs actually were. We did not look to the expense of the television airtime, we trusted God, and obeyed Him every step of the way. God told us to purchase TV cameras.

••• MEDITATIVE THOUGHT •••

Your mind is a prophet.

We bought the best state-of-the-art cameras that money could buy back then, with our small congregation. With just one hundred and fifty members we raised $170,000.00 and purchased all our own TV equipment with cash. How could we do that? Most churches that had thousands of members were not doing that. We didn't have any rich underwriters in our church paying all of the bills for us. Though the parishioners were not rich in fact, they were rich in truth. And that really was all that mattered.

Raising that kind of money was a miracle. Launching a national television broadcast with a shoestring budget was also a miracle. To this day, I still don't know how we did it. God within us did it. Nonetheless it was a miracle. Those kinds of miracles are the fragments from my past that I continually rehearse over and over again in my mind. If God came through for me, I am certain that you are next in line for a miraculous blessing. That's my testimony and I'm sticking to it!

CHAPTER FOUR

Imago Dei—The Wisdom of God's Image

And God said, Let us make man in our image, after our likeness: and let them have dominion over the fish of the sea, and over the fowl of the air, and over the cattle, and over all the earth, and over every creeping thing that creepeth upon the earth. So God created man in his own image, in the image of God created he him; male and female created he them. And God blessed them, and God said unto them, Be fruitful, and multiply, and replenish the earth, and subdue it: and have dominion over the fish of the sea, and over the fowl of the air, and over every living thing that moveth upon the earth. Genesis 1:26–28

You are God's reflection. There is no one on earth who looks more like God than you do. Tragically, you have lived the greater part of your entire life wearing a mask, a royal disguise. For the sake of pleasing the others you have traded your God given face in exchange for an impersonator's image. Who is this impersonator whose image you have taken upon yourself?

And the third angel followed them, saying with a loud voice, If any man worship the beast and his image, and receive his mark in his forehead, or in his hand, The same shall drink of the wine of the wrath of God, which is poured out without mixture into the cup of his indignation; and he shall be tormented with fire and brimstone in the presence of the holy angels, and in the presence of the Lamb. Revelation 14:9–10

••• MEDITATIVE THOUGHT •••

You are God's reflection

The image of the beast is any thought process that directly opposes and contradicts God's thoughts. Notice that the Bible says that the image of the beast would be identified by the sight of a mark on the forehead (the place of man's/God's thoughts and imagination) or in his hand (the place of service and worship). So then, a person possesses the spirit of the anti-Christ when he or she embraces any other thought than the thoughts which God has established in His Word.

The hand represents the part that gives your thoughts their worth or worth-ship. The works of man's hand, giving the thoughts approval or affirmation, carries out the thoughts that are manufactured in the mind. Man's thoughts must be carefully guarded against other-minded ideas as to preserve the posterity of your inheritance. That is why the Bible says that you should cast down vain imaginations.

Casting down imaginations, and every high thing that exalteth itself against the knowledge of God, and bringing into captivity every thought to the obedience of Christ. 2 Corinthians 10:5

Who knows more, you or God? Obviously God's wisdom is greater than the wisdom of man. However, when man's fleshly reasoning gets introduced into the scheme of things, it usually tries to logicize why God said what He said instead of simply accepting it as is. Your meditations should be solely centered upon His Word and His thoughts toward you, not human theology. Whatever God says you are, you are; whether or not anyone can actually agree. *For I know the thoughts that I think toward you, saith the LORD, thoughts of peace, and not of evil, to give you an expected end. (Jeremiah 29:11)*

••• MEDITATIVE THOUGHT •••

The image of the beast is any thought process that directly opposes and contradicts God's thoughts.

God sent the prophet Samuel to the young lad, David, who was chosen from all of Jesse's sons to be anointed king. Who would have thought David would have qualified to become king over Israel? To look upon his external image and to look at his experience, he clearly did not qualify for such a lofty appointment. The common thought was that the first-born should be king. Jesse's first-born son, Eliab, looked far more qualified to become a king than his younger sibling David. However, David was God's choice not man's. Even the prophet did not immediately go to David.

When everybody in society accepts a certain way of thinking as normal, whoever chooses to become a contrarian to conventional thoughts then becomes a pariah. You must make up in your mind that you will proudly wear the image of God. The very image of God carries with it great wisdom. When you meditate on the things that matter most to God, not only will you become prosperous, you will also be established. Choose now to follow hard after God's image. You may not be popular with man, but you will certainly be a friend of God.

MEDITATING ON PROSPERITY

Prosperity is a thought created in the mind of God. You may wonder why a thread line consistent throughout this work continues to deal with prosperity. There are too many people, including believers, who struggle with the idea that God wants them to be prosperous and excel in their health in direct proportion to their soul's prosperity. *(see 3 John 2)*. Not knowing, and being fully convinced that this is God's will for them, they flirt with poverty falsely thinking that poverty is some kind of spiritual virtue.

```
••• MEDITATIVE THOUGHT •••

Prosperity is a thought created
in the mind of God.
```

Poverty is an imbalance in your life, and God hates a false balance. Despite your background or upbringing, it is not God's will for you to be poor. The very root of poverty is birthed out of bad religion. This bad theology has become so pervasive that most people generally agree that God would rather people live with very little or even do without. The problem with this doctrine is that it has become so mainstream that people began to meditate on that false teaching rather than the Word of the Lord.

For centuries, bondage religion has used scare tactics swathed in the "any moment rapture" and "Jesus is coming soon" theology to produce an entire church of lethargic and lackadaisical followers. I know very intelligent people who were young, twenty or thirty years ago, who refused to go to college and earn a degree because they thought that Jesus was coming soon, so they didn't bother to waste their time. Several decades later Jesus hasn't returned and they still haven't earned a college degree.

••• MEDITATIVE THOUGHT •••

What you meditate on is what you get.

This escapist theology is not a new message at all. It has been around for 2,000 years. What should you do then? You must live as if Christ is coming today, but at the same time plan as if He's not coming for another 2,000 years. You must seize prosperity now. What you meditate on is what you get. The reason why there is so much poverty among us is because poverty exists in the consciousness of mankind. When you replace thoughts of poverty with thoughts of wealth, wealth will appear. Whatever you think will be empowered by Spirit to come to pass.

Contrary to what the church has taught, poverty has nothing to do with holiness. If poverty represented holiness, then God would be one of the biggest sinners and charlatans of all time. God created a heaven with streets of gold. Paving the streets with gold is a definite characteristic of lavish living, not paucity. The outgrowth of prosperity is not only identified in dollars and cents, but can also be seen in terms of health. Health is wealth. However, in order for a person to be totally healthy they will have to adopt healthy habits, first of which are healthy thoughts on which to meditate.

Again, the greater task is to renounce bad theology and replace it with proper thinking. The church has taught that when sickness comes in an individual, God is trying to teach them a lesson. That really doesn't make much sense. People still tend to believe that way despite how ridiculous it sounds. If God really was the one who put sickness on a person, then why ask anyone to pray for you, that would only be out of God's will. Many people who are sick will remain that way until they become aware that the healer lives within them.

> ••• MEDITATIVE THOUGHT •••
>
> *Living prosperously should be*
> *your daily meditation.*

So to pray to a God somewhere in the ethereal realm, in outer space, is not proper. That is why your prayers will not get answered. You must go within. He that is joined unto God is one spirit. The presence of God in one place does not mean that He is absent in another. God is ubiquitous—He is everywhere at the same time. What does God have to say about prosperity? What does God believe about your healing? **What He believes is what you must meditate on.** Whatever you define as living prosperously should be your daily meditation.

That may look like this: having a loving relationship with the love of your life, experiencing perfectly divine health, never getting sick at all, and having more than enough finances for you to meet all of your obligations and to help others in the process as well. For you prosperity may be funding a mission in Africa, or financing an orphanage in Peru. Maybe you will feel very prosperous if you raised money to find a cure for AIDS. Perhaps helping displaced Israelis to get back home to Israel is what drives your passion. Prosperity looks different from one person to the next. However you define prosperity is fine, just be sure to allow the dominant image of those thoughts to be a perpetual prop before your mental image.

THE MASTER PLANNER

God is the master planner. Since you are made in the image of God you too should be a skilled planner.

God does not do things haphazardly. The Bible teaches that God planned all things. Everything that God created was first in His mind as an organized thought before it became a manifested reality. The heavens and the earth were both planned creations. The beasts of the field as well as humanity were all planned in the mind of God. Even before Adam fell, God had a plan for the fall and a plan for his restoration. The marriage supper of the lamb was planned thousands of years ahead of schedule.

> ••• MEDITATIVE THOUGHT •••
>
> *Everything that God created was first in His mind as an organized thought before it became a manifested reality.*

Before you arrived here on earth, God sat you down and informed you of everything that you were going to pass through in this realm. Then He sent you back to earth and deleted your quondam memory so you could experience and work your way through all of the various stages of life. So then, why are you here and what was God's plan? You were sent here to become a repairer of the breach. Some people do not have a prosperity problem, yet they have a breach problem. You've breached or violated your contract with God.

••• MEDITATIVE THOUGHT •••

You were sent to earth to become
a repairer of the breach.

To repair your breach you must come into a covenantal union with God and begin to do all things in remembrance of Him. When you do that, you will be empowered to take that which is dismembered and re-member it. Know also, that holiness also infers the idea of wholeness. True holiness is when a person is completely whole in every area of their lives. Since all men have fallen short of God's glory holiness then becomes an endless pursuit of God's image and His nature. You are never truly holy until you become completely whole. And that level of wholeness only comes when you become Christ.

In our world, we call a person a genius if they are able to use about 8% of their mind. Imagine what would happen if you knew how to tap into the remaining 92%. You would operate in full knowledge. You would operate in such full knowledge that you would no longer be. Enoch walked with God so closely until he was not. Becoming whole brings one closer to such a spiritual moment. Such an experience however does not just occur by chance or happenstance. It is intentional.

••• MEDITATIVE THOUGHT •••

True holiness is when a person is completely whole in every area of their lives.

Meditation brings you closer to the actualization of your premeditated thoughts. Through meditation you will begin to realize that God really lowered Himself and became "God" only so that we could understand Him. Before God was God, He was nothing or no thing. In the beginning there was nothing and God spoke to nothing and out of nothing came everything. That is the mystery of God. This mystery can only be discerned through meditation. The most precious things concerning God and His system will never be accessed through the natural mind.

••• MEDITATIVE THOUGHT •••

Meditation brings you closer to the actualization of your premeditated thoughts.

The keys to all of the valuable treasures that God has in store are reserved solely for the ones who meditate on Him day and night. The Apostle Paul was caught up in the third heaven hearing things that were unlawful to repeat. What was he hearing? Whatever it was he could not find the right words to articulate what he heard and saw.

*I knew a man in Christ above fourteen years ago,
(whether in the body, I cannot tell; or whether out
of the body, I cannot tell: God knoweth;) such an
one caught up to the third heaven. And I knew
such a man, (whether in the body, or out of the
body, I cannot tell: God knoweth;) How that he
was caught up into paradise, and heard
unspeakable words, which it is not lawful for a
man to utter. 2 Corinthians 12:2–4*

The Bible calls this experience that Paul had a
vision. This is actually a glimpse of what focused
meditation really looks like. The practice of planning
actually produces the atmosphere conducive for
your meditations to be birthed in this sphere. Have
you ever seen a skyscraper built without first having
plans beforehand? Has anyone ever gotten rich
without having a plan set in place? Does any person
ever fulfill his or her goals in life without the aid of
an intelligent plan? The answer to all of these
questions is no. As God plans, so should you.

But know this, that if you do not plan, you
really do not have anything to contemplate in
your mind. You have nothing to meditate on.

Some people foolishly believe that to plan, to save money, or to make preparations for the future, resembles faithlessness. That is totally untrue. When you plan you are actually sending out a message to the universe that you are acting in faith, and trusting spirit to bring all things into being. And it is those plans that you write down, review and ponder on, that become your most dominant thoughts with which you create your future.

> ••• MEDITATIVE THOUGHT •••
>
> *The practice of planning actually produces the atmosphere conducive for your meditations to be birthed in this sphere.*

YOUR "I AM" NATURE

One of the most vital connections to your meditation moments is in knowing who you are. You have been told that you were everything other than who you really are. If you were reared in an environment where you were always berated and talked down to, then you were probably told all negative things about yourself, causing you to feel insecure and unworthy. On the other end, you may have been reared in a home where people affirmed you and told you wonderful things about yourself. They told you that you would be a lawyer, doctor, athlete, or a famous entertainer.

••• MEDITATIVE THOUGHT •••

The most vital connections to your meditation moments are in knowing who you are.

While that is not a bad thing to encourage someone in his or her pursuits in life, it is not best. Don't settle for good when you can have great. The best knowledge anyone can pass on to you is that you are the personification of god. God's name is I AM and since you are His child your name is I AM. When a person knows that they are God in principle they go through life with a certain aura of excellence and high expectation. This person does not settle for just anything in life because they expect the best.

God's name is I AM and since you are
His child your name is I AM.

They get what they imagine. Take a look around your town, your city, or in certain neighborhoods. Who lives in the finest homes, drives the latest automobiles, sends their children to the finest schools, eats at the finest restaurants, and gives liberally to the charity of their choice? It is the people who *expect* to live on a certain level of life, people who believe within themselves that they are God. Now if you were to approach them and ask them, "Do you really think you are God?" They would probably deny it, knowing that you couldn't handle the truth.

When a person knows that they are God
in principle they go through life
with a certain aura of excellence
and high expectation.

But in all reality they really don't have to confess it when they know it. Throughout the scriptures God declared repeatedly I AM GOD. The reason why He said this is not for His benefit but rather for the benefit of the people to whom He was speaking. They needed to know who He was and is so that they could draw spiritual blessings from the Lord. If you don't know where the bank is, you cannot make a withdrawal. If you don't know where the supermarket is, you will not be able to purchase groceries. If you don't know who God is, then you will not know where to find help when you need it. So when God says I AM GOD it is for you to know who He is for your profit.

People who walk around on earth as if they are God do so, not for your benefit, so then they really do not have to announce who they are. They simply live out their lives in a position of control and power. Only two people will have a problem with you when you begin to declare your "I AM" status. The first person who will have a problem with your knowledge of self are obviously those who believe that they are God, and they've made no more room for anyone else. The other people who will be mad at you are those people who are subjects or subjugated by the oppressor.

••• MEDITATIVE THOUGHT •••

I AM GOD

The oppressor does not want you to rise up to your rightful place in life, and neither does his subjects. Thanks be unto God, that the choice is not up to anyone other than yourself. You choose to become. You must declare that you are I AM. God revealed various facets or faces of Himself to men such as Noah; Abraham, the father of faith; Isaac, the son of promise; and Jacob, who would later become Israel. He revealed to them His various expressions of Himself, El Shaddai—the many breasted one, Jehovah Jireh—the Lord who provides, and Jehovah Rapha—the Lord our Healer, just to name a few.

••• MEDITATIVE THOUGHT •••

The oppressor does not want you to rise up to your rightful place in life, and neither do his subjects.

It wasn't until Moses, the lawgiver and deliverer, came on the scene that God actually revealed Himself as I AM. God was saying to Moses, whatever you want me to be I AM that. So when you become renewed, you then become a partaker of Christ's divine nature and you become I AM. I AM is your name. One of the great spiritual minds and mystics Meister Eckhart grasped a deep revelation in Galatians 2:20 which says, *"I am crucified with*

Christ: nevertheless I live; yet not I, but Christ liveth in me: and the life which I now live in the flesh I live by the faith of the Son of God, who loved me, and gave himself for me."

From that, Meister Eckhart said these words: "My me is God," referring to *Christ liveth in me.* That may sound a bit strange at first but just read it. My me, is God. Your me is God. "I" represents God. In other words, that I AM is the only God there is. Me is the equivalent to I AM. What he was trying to convey is that you are one, in complete union with I AM. Since this is true, your entire life should reflect one of complete unification with God. It's a spiritual fusion. You can only arrive at this place of "I AM-ness" through mediation. You cannot purchase it, you really can't work for it, and you can't trade it. You just have to know it once you become aware of it.

••• MEDITATIVE THOUGHT •••

"My Me is God"

A little boy or girl is not born with the full understanding of their sexuality. As he or she grows they become aware and then take on the nature of that which they are aware of within themselves. On this level of consciousness there is no devil. The only devil that exists in your life is the one you willingly chose. Jesus said, *"Hereafter I will not talk much with you: for the prince of this world cometh, and hath nothing in me." (John 14:30)* The prince of this world has no hold on you.

••• MEDITATIVE THOUGHT •••

Your entire life should reflect, one of complete unification with God.

The only way the devil can enter into your being is when you invite him into your consciousness through the words I AM, your god nature. When you say I AM sick, sickness has to appear because God spoke it and it must come to pass. Whenever you declare I AM broke, you will be poor. Whatever you attach to I AM is what you will have. I AM are the most powerful words in your spiritual vocabulary. I AM reveals not only your present identity but also your future position. I AM is the secret password into the realm of your soul. One cannot know true meditation without understanding the power of the words I AM—the true nature of God in you.

MIND THERAPY

That ye put off concerning the former conversation the old man, which is corrupt according to the deceitful lusts; And be renewed in the spirit of your mind. Ephesians 4:22–23

Throw off your old sinful nature and your former way of life, which is corrupted by lust and deception. Instead, let the Spirit renew your thoughts and attitudes. 24 Put on your new nature, created to be like God—truly righteous and holy. Ephesians 4:22–24 New Living Translation, © Tyndale House Publishers

Why was your old sinful nature worth throwing off? It is because sin means that you have missed the mark, and until you cast off your old nature, your old mindset, you will continue to miss the mark. How can one tell that they have truly rid themselves of the old and have now embraced the new? Your conversation, the words you speak, will reveal more about you and what you are thinking than anything else. When you have truly embraced the Zoë life—the God kind of life, you will no longer attribute any negative to I AM. That transformation comes through the passages of your mind.

You must train your mind to think differently about everything, especially to what things you will respond to in life. Your responses to life's circumstances will determine your outcome. There are always two things that will motivate you in life at all times. Those two things are pain and pleasure. Both pain and pleasure come from the same source. One is "evening" and the other is "morning." You need them both because together they make day.

And God called the light Day, and the darkness he called Night. And the evening and the morning were the first day. Genesis 1:5

••• MEDITATIVE THOUGHT •••

*You must train your mind to think
differently about everything, especially
to what things you will respond to in life.*

Both pain and pleasure are the master motivators. In fact, they are the only motivators. You should not look at either one as a negative thing. Pain is simply an indication that you need an adjustment somewhere in your life. Usually that adjustment is most needed in the area of your thinking. Pain is an indicator of the things you've been meditating on. When it arrives, you become quickly self-motivated to find any means necessary to silence its voice, or to just deal with it long enough for it to become pleasurable for you.

That is why some people choose to live in painful situations. You look at them and wonder how in the world could they live like that? They have trained their minds to feel good about a not-so-good situation. It's all in the mind. Have you ever seen people go back into an abusive relationship after being released from it? The reason why is because they have become so accustomed to being abused, that they cannot function in society without that kind of abusiveness happening to them. The abuse has become a comfortable thing in their mind.

••• MEDITATIVE THOUGHT •••

Both pain and pleasure are the master motivators. In fact, they are the only motivators.

They are not hurting badly enough yet to make the move out of that situation. They haven't experienced enough pain. That may seem strange to you, but everyone has a different threshold for pain. Everyone's tolerance levels differ. The only way for a person like this to be free is to get mind therapy. And in mind therapy you start to understand the powerful concept of "image." It's no accident that the words image and imagination are so closely connected. When you develop an awareness of God's image in you, your imagination will blossom.

When you understand the image of God you begin to realize that you are actually mandated to respond to certain situations in the same way that God would. How does God respond to tragedy, loss, poverty, defeat, and betrayal? In reality He really doesn't respond to it at all. God can only give what He is. He cannot respond to poverty because poverty is not in His consciousness. He cannot respond to sickness because He doesn't have any point of reference. God has never been sick.

••• MEDITATIVE THOUGHT •••

When you develop an awareness of God's image in you, your imagination will blossom.

So then, He can only offer what He is. God is healing. He is riches, faithfulness, excellence, victory and joy unspeakable. So if that is who

God is, if those things reflect the image of God, then God can only be those things. When you come into the fullness of this Word from the Lord, you will then understand why one person can lose their job making millions of dollars at a Fortune 500 company and allow that pain to motivate them to become richer in the process, while another person can lose his or her job making forty-five thousand dollars, and decide to commit suicide.

One person understands image, at least on some level. And you can tell by the inner fortitude to get back up and try again that they are using pain for the purpose it was created, to move you forward in life. Pain was never designed to kill you but rather to reveal you. How you respond to pain tells me what you are made of, and also what you meditate on each day. It tells me everything I need to know about your character. It lets me know whether you are a quitter or a winner in life. A person who loses everything and gets it all back plus more in a month's time lets me know that they meditate on prosperity so frequently that even a loss cannot set them back.

Whatever you meditate on will always show up, even if you have a setback. If you lived everyday for the past ten years training your mind in psychotherapy to "think and grow rich," reading Napoleon Hill's *The Laws of Success*, Bishop Jordan's *The Laws of Thinking* and *The Business of Getting Rich*, and Wallace Wattles' *The Science of Getting Rich*, you will inevitably have to win. You could lose everything in the stock market yet somehow you will soon rise again to become an investment giant, because you have read and listened only to the things that pertain to wealth.

••• MEDITATIVE THOUGHT •••

Pain was never designed to kill you but rather to reveal you.

Do you think that a Rockefeller could be poor? Well anything is possible, but that is highly improbable. Why is that? Even the fifth generation Rockefeller understands the image of John D.

Rockefeller, the patriarchal father of the Standard Oil Company. They know that they have been born into such an affluent dynasty. By simply being born into the Rockefeller family, the image of Rockefeller affords you a certain lifestyle that the commoner knows not of. In the same manner, when you have been born of the water and of the spirit, you no longer look like your former life but have now been grafted into a new bloodline— Imago Dei, the image of God.

Jesus came to this earth remembering who He was. You came into the earth forgetting who you were. You forgot in whose image you were made, thus you did not know how to think on your heritage. Know this, you have a spiritual heritage whose bloodline traces back to Jesus Christ, to David, all the way to father Abraham, to God. Just knowing that, and pondering over that truth will jump-start the process of renewal in your soul.

Pray this meditative prayer:

Father God in me, allow me to always see God within. I will not look outside of myself to find

God, but will rather seek the kingdom of God that eternally exists inside of me. I will speak to the "I AM" in me. And, I will only attach my me, my "I AM," to the things that are worthy of being connected to such a sacred name. Amen.

CHAPTER FIVE

Mysteries Unveil Ignorance

And he said unto them, Unto you it is given to know the mystery of the kingdom of God: but unto them that are without, all these things are done in parables: That seeing they may see, and not perceive; and hearing they may hear, and not understand; lest at any time they should be converted, and their sins should be forgiven them. Mark 4:11–12

It is essential that you allow the Word of God to become a part of your life through mediation. So many people say, "I read the Bible every day." "I've read the Bible through in one year." That is fine, however just reading the Bible alone will not afford you the spiritual prowess that only comes through meditation. There are many theological scholars who are well learned and highly knowledgeable concerning the history of Jesus. They can tell you everything about where Jesus lived, where he grew up, and even what kind of chores he did when he was a lad.

Biblical archaeologists can take you to the exact points in history where major events occurred. They will show you mountains, temples, rivers, oceans, and ruins. They are experts on the history of scripture. But if you ask any one of them to dialogue with you about the mysteries of Christ, most of them would become dumbfounded by the inquiry. You must go beyond the history of Jesus onto the mystery of the living Christ. In order to do that, to find out the mysteries of Christ, you have to meditate on the word not just read it.

••• MEDITATIVE THOUGHT •••

You must go beyond the history of Jesus onto the mystery of the living Christ.

It is during meditation that your mind becomes renewed. Some people believe that if they just go to church every Sunday and listen to the minister sermonize them, they will eventually become renewed in their mind. Sunday services alone will never renew your mind. It is what you do between services that determines what you will inherit and whether or not your mind will be transformed. Although what you hear has a great deal to do with your mind being renewed, hearing alone does not produce results. Hearing produces faith. Results are produced only when you take action. It is hearing and rehearsing that which you have heard that will cause you to take action. This is the law of repetition.

••• MEDITATIVE THOUGHT •••

Just going to Sunday services alone will never renew your mind.

Meditation is not simply a practice that you perform every now and then. It is a daily service. You do it until it becomes a part of you. Meditation is a lifestyle. If you breathed air last week through your nostrils, would that intake of fresh oxygen last you until next week Thursday? It would not. In the same manner the human body needs oxygen in order to live, the spirit of man must meditate in sacred communion with God in order to survive. Perhaps you think, "There are so many people who are spiritual yet they don't meditate, are they merely subsisting?"

••• MEDITATIVE THOUGHT •••

Meditation is not simply a practice that you perform every now and then. Meditation is a lifestyle.

Actually anyone who does not practice meditation is hanging on for dear life yet does not know it. The person who does not take the time to meditate is generally the one who rely upon the work of their flesh to produce the results they desire. Work is all right. However, there comes a point in time where you must cease from your labor and then allow spirit to take over from there. There are some things that you, in and of yourself, will never be able to do in this lifetime; only spirit can do it.

When you have reached the end of your rope and you have seemingly run out of options, that is when you should allow spirit to take over and carry you the rest of the way. There are so many spiritual leaders today who are suffering from anxiety, unnecessary pressure, hypertension, and even nervous breakdowns. The reason is that they have taken on loads that they were not able to handle. They built buildings that they could not afford, took on television airtime expense that were far above their ability to pay, and depended solely on the people to make it happen.

> ••• MEDITATIVE THOUGHT •••
>
> *There comes a point in time where you must cease from your labor and then allow spirit to take over from there.*

Don't misunderstand me; there is nothing wrong with stretching in faith to get things that you ordinarily would never have. When you stretch, that pleases God because it is faith in action. What you must understand is that after you have stretched, it is then up to God to finance your faith. The way that is done is by going into your secret closet and closing the door and meditating until the answer comes specifically for your assignment. If God told you to build a 4000-seat cathedral, then build it. But the way you are going to pay for it is not by asking the people. It goes way beyond that obvious approach.

You may get some money that way, but not all of it. The bigger the vision that God has placed in your hand, the more expansive your meditation should be. God gives you the complete blueprint, the how-to's in your meditation. How will you pay for the house, fill up the cathedral, pay off the tuitions, cut your debts, purchase the right stock, or go into the perfect business? You'll find out the answers when you meditate. Maybe God will show you what he showed me. God told me to "Grow the people." He assured me that if I grew the people that I would never have to worry about how I would pay for anything.

Many leaders are really concerned about growing their churches numerically, but don't spend substantial time growing the people. That is why they live in a continual deficit. I would have never thought of that on my own. It was in my meditation time that God taught me the principle of Jesus in growing disciples. He taught me how to weigh my members instead of counting them. That was a life-changing revelation for me. Meditation always brings about revelation. Just because you meditate once in a while will not bring you to a point of proficiency.

Not only is meditation a lifestyle, it is also life-long. You become a master of it by understanding its artistic nature. Meditation is also an art form. Like an artistic dancer must hone his or her skills to be relevant to their supporters, and like an abstract visual artist must paint works that compel donors to fund their fanciful imaginations, the one who meditates must explore fresh approaches to entering into the silence, the place where all creation begins. Until you embrace and cultivate the art of meditation you will remain in ignorance.

There the cost of living is far too high for any thinking person to pay.

> ••• MEDITATIVE THOUGHT •••
>
> *Silence is the place where all creation begins.*

KNOWLEDGE AND IGNORANCE DO NOT AGREE

Knowledge is powerful, but can be extremely dangerous if it is not tempered with preparation. If you went to Columbia University and attended classes without ever buying a textbook, how would you ever know how to solve problems or which formula would work best for a particular problem? You wouldn't. You would be unprepared. God holds you accountable for everything that you hear. When you hear more knowledgeable truths, He expects you to grow from the truth that you hear. To ignore truth is tantamount to rejecting God. God is the embodiment of truth.

I can remember when I would ask God for more revelation knowledge of His Word. Deep down inside, I wanted to know so much more than the fundamental things that I have heard taught for decades. There were many deep mysteries in the scripture, many of which God alone knew the hidden meanings to, and I wanted that knowledge. God asked me, "Son, are you ready? Are you really ready? Do you really want to come behind the veil? Do you really want the deeper things?" Eager and anticipating, I answered, "Of course God, yes I am ready."

••• MEDITATIVE THOUGHT •••

To ignore truth is tantamount to rejecting God. For God is the embodiment of truth.

Then the Lord said, "Brace yourself, because when I start to take you deeper into the wisdom of My Spirit, I will also have to unveil ignorance." With that I knew that my whole life and ministry and perspective on things would change. As God began to reveal the wisdom in the mysteries of His Word, I became less tolerant of ignorance. In my meditations I began to see others and also myself very differently. As I crossed the threshold into new realities and ancient truths concerning the scriptures, I found that there were some people who began to be uncomfortable around me.

It wasn't anything that I personally did to them. The camaraderie between us was no longer there. That compelled me to start assessing my relationships, all of them. I began affirming to some people that there wasn't anything necessarily wrong with them, I had just grown in my understanding of the mysteries of God and came to realize that they hadn't grown with me. Even in my church there were some people that began to sense the shift in my teaching. They noticed that I was taking a totally different approach as I began to teach more on the mind of God in you.

••• MEDITATIVE THOUGHT •••

Meditation will cause you to grow in your understanding of the mysteries of God

---

As a prophet, I've never really taught messages that were shallow. There is nothing one-dimensional about the prophetic at all. Most of the people who came to the services in the early days came because they were attracted to the prophetic. That dimension of ministry is still the prevailing theme until this very day. However, when God began to add onto the existing knowledge that I was previously teaching, it made some people antsy since they had never heard such things taught before.

One of the things that I have found out about church people is that they respond much like Russian scientist Ivan Pavlov's dogs in his infamous experiment. Pavlov was examining the gastric function of dogs by externalizing the salivary gland so that he could measure how much the dogs salivated when they were hungry and what type of stimuli would cause such an action to occur. Every time he rang his dinner bell, his dogs began to secrete saliva as if they were actually eating the food. It was an automatic response.

In the same way, church folks salivate at the ringing of the bell of the scriptures with which they are familiar. Like the dogs, believers too salivate at the sound of their favorite scriptures, yet after the salivation there is no substance, no real solid food to digest. Most churchgoers have been trained to respond a certain way to what they've already heard a million times before. If I say *all things work together...* most church goers would automatically chime in, *"for good to them that love God, to them who are the called according to his purpose."* *(Romans 8:28)* The problem is that in reality nothing good is really happening to them, and that's by their own admission.

That and hundreds of other scriptures come to them like second nature. It's almost like a bunch of small children singing nursery rhymes, having a whole lot of fun dancing to the fancy tunes, but lacking the cognitive skill to properly understand what the implicit meaning is. But how about if I say, "you are God" or "there is no devil." Immediately I am looked at as a heretic, not because what I am saying is not scriptural but rather that you are unfamiliar with such phrasing. Unfortunately these "nursery rhymes," or should I say hidden mysteries, are new to you and you've not quite committed them to memory just yet.

> ••• MEDITATIVE THOUGHT •••
>
> *If you try to walk hand in hand with ignorance while trying to successfully balance knowledge, you will get dispossessed in the process.*

I would tell my congregation, "If you feel that my teaching is too straightforward and commanding, too rough for you to handle then either you are being prepared for a new level of understanding or to be evicted out of my life." Eviction happens when two do not agree. If you don't pay your landlord his or her rent on time, they will evict you because you are not in agreement. You have actually broken your agreement. If you try to walk hand in hand with ignorance while trying to successfully balance knowledge, you will get dispossessed in the process. I see it all of the time with married couples, particularly those couples who have been married ten or more years.

Married couples often divorce when one mate grows at a rate that their spouse cannot keep up with. One of them grows out of place. When you first got married you were equally yoked. You both were ignorant. Neither of you had any real of depth of understanding. Then one of you decided to submit yourself to a lifestyle of spiritual training, mentoring, and development. That is when all hell broke loose in your life. Now you are all about knowledge, the knowledge of God. But you have a problem of being completely irrelevant to one another and not on par with your spouse.

That is why it is rather dangerous to sit under high revelatory teaching ministry of the Word without your spouse. You are getting revelatory truths that are transforming your entire mind and revolutionizing your life, yet your spouse is on the same low level of consciousness on which they started. You have been enlightened to a new way of thinking that can no longer tolerate ignorance manifesting in your home. Now the battle is on.

You have higher expectations in life, since your spiritual perspective has changed.

Your spouse is on the same plateau of unawareness, the same place they've been from day one. It is obvious to you that you have embraced a better way. What isn't as apparent to you is that your spouse is an identical replica of what you were before you allowed your mind to expand. That is why the Bible asks the question:

Can two walk together, except they be agreed? Amos 3:3

I've said that some of the people in your life will get evicted. Sad to say, sometimes that person is your own spouse. At other times it may be family members or close friends. You have to evict anyone whose ignorance may prevent you from fulfilling the purposes of God in life. These people don't agree. So they've got to go. Be aware of this though; you cannot evict all of them. Some people must stay around you as a reminder to you of what you should not do. Having them around will be like a constant reminder of what you will never revert back to.

*You have to evict anyone whose ignorance
may prevent you from fulfilling the
purposes of God in life.*

Their presence will remind you to continually press forward in life and in the things of God. Having some disagreement around can be good, especially when it helps to shape your character and create a better you along the way. Jesus understood this very well, which is why He kept Apostle Thomas around who doubted and Apostle Judas who betrayed Him. Both disciples represented an element of the living Christ. Thomas reminded Christ and us also of the need to doubt; doubt your doubts, and feed your faith.

Question anything that opposes the revelation of the Christ mystery and bring it under subjection. Judas teaches us not to betray ourselves by playing to the masses in life. You shortchange yourself (about thirty pieces of silver) when you live your life trying to please the popular majority. The way of the mystic is not broad. Mystics travel a very narrow path. But in the end they find light—the knowledge of God.

> ••• MEDITATIVE THOUGHT •••
>
> *Doubt your doubts, and feed your faith.*

MEDITATION BRINGS REVELATION

Meditation has the ability to make things happen in your life. It always brings revelation. You cannot get a revelation by being in a conscious state of mind. You have to move from one state of consciousness to another. Meditation will bring you into the revelation of Christ. All of the mystics and gurus know this. You don't just come into the knowledge of Christ in a meaningful way through the efforts of your flesh; it takes meditation. Any revelation requires some form of dreaming or subconscious activity. What you dream about in the day is what you will dream about at night.

You cannot get a revelation by being in a conscious state of mind. You have to move from one state of consciousness to another.

Dreaming is that part of you that is most active in your subconscious mind. People are not usually aware in an awakened sense when they are dreaming at night. They are sleeping. They are unconscious. You hear a great deal these days about the subconscious mind. What exactly is the subconscious mind? Your subconscious mind is what drives all human behavior. It is also the area of the mind that produces manifested reality. Let me get you an illustration to show you how the subconscious mind works. Think about driving a car. At first when you start driving, every part of you is totally focused on the process of driving.

You are making sure that you are going a certain speed; you are constantly looking all around to make sure that you are in no one's way, and that no one is blocking you either. You make tons of ridiculous mistakes because driving is not natural to you yet. If you have a driving instructor in the car with you, that tends to make things worse, as you become really nervous having someone breathing down your neck, inspecting your every move. You know that if you make one wrong move that it could cost not only your life, but the lives of innocent people also.

••• MEDITATIVE THOUGHT •••

Meditation will bring you into the revelation of Christ.

So then, you make sure that you consciously do everything that you have been taught. After you learn to drive, get your drivers license, and then become experienced, the rules of the game change totally. Now when you get in the car, everything that you do, you do without thinking about it. You have been driving for years and are pretty confident now. You no longer contemplate the potholes in the road, or the stop sign near the school by your house. You just drive without really thinking about what's around you. You just do it.

You've done what you do so many times that it has become a part of your subconscious mind. The conscious mind is logical. It has to reason everything through and think it out, before it takes action. The subconscious mind is not logical at all. It does what it does without analysing the outcome. The subconscious mind already knows and expects the outcome to be a certain way. The reason it knows is because it has rehearsed the same routine over and over again in the mind. And so that which it has repeated hundreds of times becomes normal to fulfill.

••• MEDITATIVE THOUGHT •••

Your subconscious mind is what drives all human behavior. It is also the area of the mind that produces manifested reality.

So then meditation has a connection to dreams. When one meditates, you get out of your conscious mind and move into the subconscious mind. Meditation would be another aspect of directive dreaming. The distinction here is that in a dream the images direct you. In meditation you direct the dream. I cover in great detail the whole topic of dreams and visions in my work *Dreams And Visions: Letters From God and How To Read Them*. So meditation gives you more control over the outcome of your desire. However both require altered states of consciousness.

I know that some believers get all bent out of shape when I speak of altered states of consciousness. Most Pentecostals ascribe to the concept of altered states of consciousness even if they don't realize it. The whole phenomenon of glossolalia, which is speaking in unknown heavenly tongues, requires an altered state of consciousness. Along with that experience are also experiences such as singing in tongues, dancing in the spirit, and even many forms of divine healing. All of those are altered states.

*When one meditates, you get out of your
conscious mind and move into
the subconscious mind.*

For now I want you to understand that when a
person gets a revelation from God, that revelation
comes when you are in meditation, having a dream
or seeing a vision. It has to come in one of these
ways because God never speaks in the loudness.
He always speaks when things are still and
peaceful. That is another reason why meditation
is so important, it sends a message to God that
you are ready to receive directions from heaven.
Regardless of how chaotic your life is, you have
disciplined yourself to take a moment to refrain
from the madness and get in serious touch with
God. God generally honors that by giving you a
word that will change your situation and your
whole life forever.

```
┌─────────────────────────────────────┐
│                                       │
│      ••• MEDITATIVE THOUGHT •••       │
│                                       │
│   Meditation is an aspect of directive│
│     dreaming. In a dream the images   │
│       direct you. In meditation you   │
│           direct the dream.           │
│                                       │
└─────────────────────────────────────┘
```

INTO THE DARKNESS

Darkness is the place of unformed purpose—
Bishop E. Bernard Jordan

Don't be afraid of the dark. In order for you to tap into the hidden treasures buried inside, you have to go within. You are going to have to get in touch with your most inner self. Although people claim to be lovers of the truth, most people could not handle the real truth about themselves, so they hide. They do not want to go within, because that is where the truth lies. The truth, your solution, your riches, and your blessings all live in the darkest place on earth—within you.

Don't despair. The truth takes form in darkness.
Many people are afraid of dark places because
they have heard rumors about dreadful things that
happen in the dark. They trip up over things in the
dark. They stagger when they walk, afraid that
they might hurt themselves. Being in darkness
is an ultimate test of your faith. You can't see
anything, but you are still expected to trust and
obey God. You are nervous. You don't want to
touch the wrong thing. Worse yet, you don't want
the wrong thing touching you.

... MEDITATIVE THOUGHT ...

Being in darkness is an ultimate test of your faith. You can't see anything, but you are still expected to trust and obey God.

Regardless of all the logical arguments to avoid the darkness, you must stay there until you become. It is in the darkness, in meditation, that you truly find out who you are. You come face to face with the real you. Sometimes there are things about yourself that you are not ready to deal with. In the darkness you discover feelings of hate, greed, jealously, and vengeance. Perhaps you struggle with trusting others. It is in darkness that you face these harsh realities.

Meditation brings about revelation. Of course, you want to get to the great revelations first: the blessings, the money, good health, and success. There is nothing wrong with that. Truth is that you will at least have to deal with the dark side first, those things within you that were preventing you from having your desires in the first place. Once you deal with those things, tapping into the others won't be an issue. In fact, it'll be as easy as driving a car.

SOARING TO HIGH PLACES

> ••• MEDITATIVE THOUGHT •••
>
> *He maketh my feet like hinds' feet,*
> *and setteth me upon my high places.*
> *—Psalms 18:33*

High achievers have very few friends. It doesn't matter what area of life you made your achievements in, you will not be welcomed by millions of like-minded fellows. Achievers travel in small packs. If you want to know where a person is going in life, take an assessment of their friends. Who are they hanging around? Who do they talk on the phone with every day? Who's houses are they hanging out at on the weekends? Who's coming over to their house for dinner? Meditation brings revelation and then manifestation. You will never receive your reward when you are overly concerned about who can or cannot join you in the celebration.

••• MEDITATIVE THOUGHT •••

High achievers have very few friends.

It's true, it can be lonely at the top. Even lonelier is the in-between point, the point between where you start and your intended destination. It's very crowded at the bottom. If you are with the crowd then you are at the bottom. Why is it that mansions are usually isolated on massive acreages, while the housing projects and tenements are crowded, with low-income dwellers packed in like sardines in a can? The further you descend to the bottom, the more crowded it will be. One thing is for sure: you'll have plenty of company down there; however, you won't make a difference in life.

When you begin to meditate you become isolated unto higher purposes. It is not that you are full of conceit and pride. In meditation, you have discovered your higher calling, your true purpose in life. And now that you know what that is, you "on purpose" live your life welcoming only the ones who will help you to succeed at becoming your optimal self. God places you in high places. The Bible says so. Therefore do not be ashamed when God elevates you to a higher purpose. Don't make excuses about your elevation. God raised Joseph from the pit where his brothers left him to wither away all the way to the palace where he became governor over Egypt.

••• MEDITATIVE THOUGHT •••

When you begin to meditate you become isolated unto higher purposes.

When Joseph had his brothers around him it would seem to the outsider as if having so many people around him was a good thing. Having too many people around your vision can threaten the vision that God has given you. When Joseph was in prison he was in his in-between state, the loneliest place he'd ever experienced. It was this time in prison that actually qualified him to become a reigning official. Don't despair your in-between moments in life. Learn while you are there, and know that those moments will not last forever. Get excited because your next stop is the floor that reaches all the way to the top.

IMAGINE THIS

Imagination is more important than knowledge. For while knowledge defines all we currently know and understand, imagination points to all we might yet discover and create. –Albert Einstein

Imagination is the mirror of the soul. You are God's imagination. Everything that you would ever want to be in life, God already is. And God is trying to show you how to become. The principle way to become is by imagining yourself there. Where is there? There is wherever you want it to be. You have to see yourself where you desire to be in life. Stop identifying yourself as a human being. God has never made a human being. You are not being anything. You are who you are. Labels only limit your ability to imagine.

> ••• MEDITATIVE THOUGHT •••
>
> *Imagination is the mirror of the soul.*

You start believing the labels put on you and then you never rise above the limitations of the label. You have never heard Mercedes Benz referred to as a car being. It's a car. It is a method of transport. You are no more a human being than you are a car. Your human personality is merely the vehicle that transports your soul. You are much more than your physical body. In fact, your body is not you. Say now, "I AM not my body." When you falsely believe that you are your body, you become body bound. Imagination, which can be practiced while meditating, will enable you to transport yourself from one situation to another.

Through imagination you will be able to lift yourself out of the doldrums of a dejected society into the holy of holies, the place where you rightfully belong. You must first see yourself as getting up and walking away from your limiting situation. It is not hard to do. All you have to do is imagine yourself getting up and walking. Your imagination will give you the supernatural power to defy the facts as you ever so passionately kiss the truth of who you are, and who you imagine yourself to be.

Whether is it easier to say to the sick of the palsy, Thy sins be forgiven thee; or to say, Arise, and take up thy bed, and walk? But that ye may know that the Son of man hath power on earth to forgive sins, (he saith to the sick of the palsy,) I say unto thee,

Arise, and take up thy bed, and go thy way into thine house. Mark 2:9–11 (bold is author's own)
Imagine Yourself There!

CHAPTER SIX

The Enemy Within

Now the Lord is that Spirit: and where the Spirit of the Lord is, there is liberty. 2 Corinthians 3:17

There are many people who miss the presence of God, or who miss what God is doing all together, because they refuse to see correctly. Dwelling on the inside of you is a universe. You never meet your enemy for the first time on this dimension, in this earthly realm; you first meet him within yourself. When you deal with the enemy within yourself, you concurrently deal with the enemy on the outside. In fact, when you deal with the enemy within, you cause the enemy outside of yourself to fade away.

When you are defeated in life it is not because the so-called devil was after you. Your defeat is due to mental blindness and moral deviations. Whatever you cannot see you cannot have. If you do not behold it you will not hold it. If you cannot see it you will not receive it. If you do not believe it you will never achieve it. Your physical eyes are only windows from which you look at things. You really see and have perception with your mind. Whatever you need to see must be seen with your mind's eye.

The eyes of your understanding being enlightened; that ye may know what is the hope of his calling, and what the riches of the glory of his inheritance in the saints. Ephesians 1:18

If you desire to have a larger income, you have to give yourself a raise mentally. If you want a bigger home, then you have got to sleep in that house, in the recesses of your mind. There is no enemy outside of yourself that is stopping you from reaching your potential in life. So when you start believing that anything other than you is holding back your forward progress, then you are really living in deception. It's all YOU. It always has been YOU. An idol god is something that is other than the Father. Anything other than the Father is otherness.

Thou shalt have no other gods before me.
Exodus 20:3

So when you are moving in otherness, you have participated in idolatry.

Thus saith the LORD the King of Israel, and his redeemer the LORD of hosts; I am the first, and I am the last; and beside me there is no God.
Isaiah 44:6

You cannot exist beside Him. God must be in you and you in God. You are what you see. The inner picture that you have of yourself has already produced the outer picture that everyone else sees. If you have a problem with the way you look, don't bother getting an exterior makeover. What you need is a mental makeover. You must be cleansed from the sickness in your mind. You suffer from a mental disease. Perhaps you are thinking, I have no mental problems at all. Well, poverty is a mental disease. To feel that poverty is acceptable in your life or in the life of any person is a mental concern. There is nothing about poverty that is good. So to welcome it on any level is a clear sign that the mind is sick and needs to recover from its traumatized state of shock.

Imagine if civil rights leaders Malcolm X and Rev. Dr. Martin Luther King Jr. were able to teach African Americans about the spiritual side of economic empowerment. Such a teaching would have revolutionized a people. Black people today would not be suffering in the impoverished conditions that many of them suffer. They would be free from the bondages of lack and paucity. The reason why they would be free is because they would have been taught how to cleanse their mind of the mental images that have held them back far too long.

Those images are images that suggest that people of color are second-class citizens unworthy of participating in a more large-scale capitalistic arena. Malcolm of course taught how to build communities economically by supporting African American businesses within the community. Seemingly no one was really listening. Not enough people were listening. The Jewish people do understand this principle and do practice it all of the time. The Asians do it. But for people of color, it's going to take some time to really grasp this freedom concept. What Dr. King and Malcolm X did for the cause of humanity was great, and I honor them.

However they both confronted the system here in the United States. I can tell you that the reason we are in the situation that we are in is not because of a system but rather the systematic programming of our minds. If you change your thinking you change your lifestyle. When you move up mentally then the chains of slavery will no longer bind you. You become whatever your mind envisions. That which you meditate upon becomes a part of your life and your experience.

This book of the law shall not depart out of thy mouth; but thou shalt meditate therein day and night, that thou mayest observe to do according to all that is written therein: for then thou shalt make thy way prosperous, and then thou shalt have good success. Joshua 1:8

Knowing this, what will you choose to see? What you see is not a forced thing. No one can make you see what you do not want to see. You can only see that which you allow your mind's eye to see. Psychoanalyst Victor Frankl, the holocaust survivor and author of the highly acclaimed book, *Man's Search for Meaning*, did not see the atrocities of dead bodies and tortured Jews in the concentration camps in Germany. Had he seen those things he too would have died. But he chose to focus on inanimate objects all around him and see the beauty in them.

••• MEDITATIVE THOUGHT •••

You can only see that which you allow your mind's eye to see.

Those objects and various things in nature became the anchor on which he based his whole philosophy of life. They became the things that made him look forward to life, by seeing the goodness in them. What are you choosing to see? Frankl in fact saw people tortured to death. But in truth he saw himself totally free from Nazi control, sharing his story of hope with untold millions of people. Seeing is a choice.

TIME TRAVEL

And God called the light Day, and the darkness he called Night. And the evening and the morning were the first day. Genesis 1:5

The day is your awake state. The night is your sleep state. At night you literally move in God, since your spirit never sleeps. In other words you actually travel in time. Every dream causes your mind to attend an event. That which is on the inside of you is infinite. That which is unlimited is trapped in that which is limited. The thing that is causing your inability to walk or move forward in life, even in a spiritual sense, is directly connected to your meditative thoughts.

••• MEDITATIVE THOUGHT •••

Every dream causes your mind to attend an event.

What you meditate on determines your ability to walk, run, fly, or crawl if that is what you choose to do. Lameness is a condition of the mind. That is why Jesus told the man with palsy to take up his bed and go. Jesus knew that the only thing stopping this man from walking away from his experience was his inability to think himself, to imagine himself in another place.

But that ye may know that the Son of man hath power on earth to forgive sins, (then saith he to the sick of the palsy,) Arise, take up thy bed, and go unto thine house. And he arose, and departed to his house. Matthew 9:6–7

Meditation in its most genuine sense has much to do with time travel. In your imagination you can literally travel to places you have never been before. The only thing that will ever stop you from journeying to destinations that you choose to go is yourself. Everything that is without really does not matter. What matters the most is that which is within you. You may sabotage your own abilities and possibilities by falsely believing that you have a potential impediment, some sort of deterrent to you reaching your highest dreams. Jesus is speaking to your lame man or lame woman and saying, "Take up your bed and walk."

The words that Jesus gave to this man in Matthew 9:6–7 were not so much words of healing as they were words of permission and release. When Jesus said those words, in the man's mind, he had the word from the Lord that would usher him into the next level of his life. That is the only thing that some people may need in life, to hear that they have permission to do, to have, and to be more than they have ever at first thought they would. The ability to transcend all boundaries in time lies within you. There is a realm in God where you can actually change matter and walk boldly through the very portals of time and space. You can walk through walls.

••• MEDITATIVE THOUGHT •••

You can actually travel in time.

Of all that you have been exposed to in terms of modern day evangelism, none has touched the surface of what is getting ready to happen. You will see a person preaching in one place, and then God will translate them to their next preaching assignment. Forget trains and planes, God's travel will be far more efficient than any other method. In order for you to tap into this time travel, you have to believe in the power of God more than anything in the world. You must believe that you can operate in that paranormal realm. Energy surrounds you. God's true state is formless. God can be anywhere at anytime because He is bound by nothing.

You too can be bound by nothing, enabling you to pass through space at warp speeds doing the unfathomable. But in order to do that, you have to be first willing to shed yourself of all of the titles that have limited your experience here in life. The more titles you receive the more you become limited. It is only when you start to pull off your titles that you will come face to face with your real identity.

AN ALLEGORY

This story tells of an old sage who carried with him a bag of gold. This wise man worked for King George. The room where the sage stood hosted many people. It was filled to capacity. The king's sage posed a challenge to the attendees at this majestic event. He said, "If anyone can identify this man, then I will reward him with the bag of gold." The first person who stepped forward to try said, "I know who he is, he is the King." The sage said, "Your answer is wrong please leave the room." The second man came in and answered saying, "Oh this man is George, that is a regal name." The sage told him to leave the room also letting him know that he had answered incorrectly.

Several others made attempts to answer this mystery question about who this man was. His wife said, "He's my husband." Someone else said, "He's a great man." Every one of them was asked to leave the room. Eventually there was no one left in the room except the king and his sage. The sage then proposed the king saying, "This gold can be yours if you can tell me who you are." The king replied, "I am your disciple; your beloved friend."

The sage told the king to leave the room. After that the sage came to the doorway, opened the door and threw the gold dust into the wind.

The king became very upset and started yelling at the sage. "Why did you throw the gold dust into the wind, do you know what you are doing?" That sage answered him saying, "I threw the dust to the wind because the wind was the only one who gave me the correct answer. The wind knew who you were." The king was furious and argued, "The wind did not say anything! I heard nothing. He did not give me a name." The sage said, "Precisely." That is who you are. Once you can be named you have lost everything, even your innate identity.

It is only when you can become nameless that you can become infinite. Once your mind has been washed thoroughly clean of all appellations, you can then become.

In the same manner of this allegorical tale, God too became limited when He stepped out of the realm called "nothingness," and man began to see Him, and label Him as God. He limited Himself to man's finite understanding of Him. You ask, "How can God be limited, after all He is God?"

> ••• MEDITATIVE THOUGHT •••
>
> *Once you can be named you have lost
> everything even your innate identity.*

You must understand that with man there is no ending to labels. That is how we live. When God is not enough then He becomes Father God, yet another limitation. When you see Him as Father God you miss out on a much needed facet of His nature as El Shaddai, the Many Breasted One.

And Adam said, This is now bone of my bones, and flesh of my flesh: she shall be called Woman, because she was taken out of Man. Therefore shall a man leave his father and his mother, and shall cleave unto his wife: and they shall be one flesh. Genesis 2:23–24

Who was Adam referring to when he said *therefore shall a man leave his father and mother?* Adam was referring to God. He knew God in a way that very few understand Him. Adam did not have any knowledge of an earthly mother or father since He was an original creation. The only way to become one with anything is to be able to leave and to cleave. You do that in consciousness. When you go behind the veil, you will no longer know Him as Father, you will just know Him.

The spirit of man is the candle of the LORD, searching all the inward parts of the belly. Proverbs 20:27

Inside of your belly you have rivers, rivers of living waters. There is a continual flow; there is a depth in you. Water is another type and form of "I AM." Water takes on the shape of whatever it is poured into. Once you can create the image in your imagination you begin to take the shape of that object. You choose between the image of poverty or prosperity. In the allegory above, one of the points you must understand is that each person called the king something different. But each person was really naming himself or herself.

They were calling the king names that they really saw within themselves. Whatever you are calling someone else; you are really calling yourself that thing. What are you calling others? The limitations that you put on others are in direct proportion to the limitations that you have placed on yourself. This is why you must distance yourself from the wrong people; the people who will not bring to the surface the things on the inside of you that must be show-cased in this hour. Your friends should bring out the best in you. The best in you has no title or status. It is pure limitless energy.

*If you can name God, then you may not know
God —Bishop E. Bernard Jordan*

THE PLANTING OF THE LORD

*And he shall be like a tree planted by the rivers of
water, that bringeth forth his fruit in his season;
his leaf also shall not wither; and whatsoever he
doeth shall prosper. Psalms 1:3*

One thing that some people do not mention
when dealing with the topic of meditation is where
one is planted. This is very important in that where
you are planted, or should I say where God plants
you, has very much to do with what you will ponder on throughout the course of your life. And
what you ponder on is directly related to the kind
of harvest you will receive in life. One area that

some people get confused about is the area of the anointing. The anointing of God does not qualify authority. Authority comes from God and ones ability to stay planted where God has rooted them.

When you are planted by the Lord, you will be able to withstand the pressures of growth, and also be able to withstand the violent storms of life without becoming uprooted. When you are truly planted by God, you are satisfied with the place that you are planted. It doesn't really matter what celebrity figure comes or goes; you will stay right where you are because you know why God placed you there. No one or no-thing can displace you because you have deep roots in the soil.

> ••• MEDITATIVE THOUGHT •••
>
> *Where God plants you has very much to do with what you will ponder on throughout the course of your life. And what you ponder on is directly related to the kind of harvest you will receive in life.*

In this I have discovered that the most unfruitful souls that I have ever seen are those who always ask questions about other people's experiences, not their own. They are busybodies. They become overly concerned with other people's plights, when at the same time their own life is swiftly falling apart. They become critical and start behaving like baby goats, balking against every self-propelling Word from God that is given. They begin to pick up a critical spirit and criticize everything they see being done. They start to tear others down to try to bring them down to the level where they are. The bottom line is that a person is either planted or they are not planted. If they are, then they have no problem getting with the program and moving forward.

One of the things that I do not do at all is bother myself with people who are shaky. For one thing, dealing with people who have no real footing will only cause you to become unstable also. It works both ways. Maybe you won't become unstable in the physical place that God has called you to be, but you will become unstable in consciousness. And God has called you to be firmly planted in consciousness.

What is consciousness? Consciousness comes from two Latin words *com* and *scire* which literally means "with knowledge." Consciousness is not only a response on an intellectual plane, but also extends to the mental and spiritual realms.

> ••• MEDITATIVE THOUGHT •••
>
> *Be careful not to deal with people*
> *who have no roots.*

Consciousness is not intellect but rather the result of the interacting between intellect and the world of matter. It is awareness. It is knowing. This knowledge however does not come from reading books and hearing teaching CD's; this kind comes only through the secret world inside of your mind. Prophet Elijah was in consciousness when God told him to go, and he went not knowing where he was going, but trusting the voice of God to take care of all his earthly needs. How did he know that he would be taken care of by ravens and that he would have a natural spring flowing from the brook Cherith? How did he know that?

COVENANT

*God has called you to be firmly
planted in consciousness.*

He didn't have a map or a navigational system to direct him to those places. Even if he did, how would he have known what would be at the place once he arrived? How did he get divinely connected with a widow woman, who was at her very last bit of resources, donates her final belongings to the prophet and then became a wealthy woman by doing so? The prophet was firmly rooted. He was planted in consciousness. He could not adequately explain this notion. At times I too have difficulty fully explaining this concept, having it make sense to a person who is not walking in it. It is what it is.

So I don't answer my critics. I do not respond to false accusations against me. To do so is to stoop to a lower level and risk the placement in consciousness where I dwell. When criticism comes against me, I rest in the knowledge and joy that I am in the right place. You don't talk about people or tear people down that are beneath you. You only reach for those who are above you. So when people do that, I know that I am above them, not in terms of a hierarchal order or some kind of caste system. No, I am above them in consciousness, which is where I am firmly planted and growing.

••• MEDITATIVE THOUGHT •••

Don't even bother responding to your critics or false accusations.

Why then is it important to be planted in the right place? Being planted where God plants you is to be rightfully connected with your blessings in life. God knows where you need to be and what you need at any given moment in time. Typically God will not plant you where you are comfortable. You will know that that is not the leading of the Lord. I hear people say, "My family left this ministry because we weren't comfortable anymore." According to the way that God thinks, that may have been the best time for you to connect and stay. When you are uncomfortable, you are growing. You are also forced to look for new ideas and concepts.

> ••• MEDITATIVE THOUGHT •••
>
> *Being planted where God plants you is to be rightfully connected with your blessings in life.*

When you are uncomfortable you begin to think and create. Some of the greatest inventions in the world came as a result when the inventors where in their most painful states. At times people produce the most ingenious masterpieces when they are confronted with insurmountable financial debts, extremely cutting deadlines, and even serious health setbacks. When you are uncomfortable with where you are planted ask yourself, "Why am I uncomfortable?"

Are you uneasy because new demands are being made and you just don't have the inner drive to meet them? Are you just comfortable with the way things always have been and you don't really want to see change? Judge your own self. Ask yourself the right questions. It may very well be that the enemy of your mind is trying to set you up to fail, removing you from the very place that God has commanded your blessing. Be Aware!

Behold, how good and how pleasant it is for brethren to dwell together in unity! It is like the precious ointment upon the head, that ran down upon the beard, even Aaron's beard: that went down to the skirts of his garments; As the dew of Hermon, and as the dew that descended upon the mountains of Zion: for there the LORD commanded the blessing, even life for evermore. Psalms 133:1–3

When you are uncomfortable you are
growing. You are also forced to search
for new ideas and concepts.

TRICK YOUR MIND

The only enemy that exists in this world is the enemy in your mind. So in order to win in life you must first conquer the battle that plagues you most often, the battle of your mind. Before you can come into wealth, peace, and prosperity you have got to trick your mind into believing that you already possess those things and that you are regularly enjoying the fruits connected with them. You have to trick your subconscious mind. The subconscious mind does not know the difference between what is real from what is not real.

So whatever you train it to believe is what it will produce for you. You have to trick your mind into believing that you are wealthy so much so that one day you will wake up and be wealthy, because your mind will not expect anything else. Years ago when I did not have much money at all, I used to go to really fancy restaurants. I could not afford to eat from the dinner menu; it was way out of my budget. So I went there during happy hour and had tea, which was all I could afford at the time. I didn't go to an all-you-can-eat buffet and just fill my stomach for $5.95. Those places are usually crowded with average thinkers.

No, I went to the most elaborate restaurants, with fancy decorum, marble floors in the vestibule, wall-to-wall custom carpeting, cherry wood walls, high cathedral ceilings, and the finest china and silverware. Everything about the surroundings suggested wealth and prosperity, and suggested the quality state that I envisioned myself on. So that is where I needed to be. I wanted to surround myself with what I should be meditating on: an environment that was consistent with my way of thinking.

It wasn't long before I was ordering food from the dinner menu. Not long after that I would take people from my church with me and pay for their meals. I had tricked my mind into believing that I could afford to eat at this restaurant and that I belonged. And guess what, it worked. My mind didn't know that I couldn't afford anything but tea. The only thing my mind knew was that I was there. And in my mind, I would not have been there at all if I weren't supposed to be there. So my mind accommodated my vast imagination and then made a way for me. It figured it out.

How does one go from a week-to-week paycheck then come into billions of dollars? That person tricked their mind into believing that they should be a billionaire rather than work a 9 to 5 job. The mind could do nothing more than just to agree with the suggestion that you gave it. When you give your mind a suggestion long enough, it hardens into a fact. And that fact then becomes the truth of God to you.

CHAPTER SEVEN

Without Form

The hearing ear, and the seeing eye, the LORD hath made even both of them. Love not sleep, lest thou come to poverty; open thine eyes, and thou shalt be satisfied with bread. Proverbs 20:12–13

As long as you are asleep you cannot see. What you must understand is that the real you is not composed of bodily parts. The real you is spirit. Your body is only an earth suit, simply a means of transporting the real you from one place to the next here in this earth realm. That is why when you die in a physical sense, your body goes back to the earth. Most people mourn the loss of what they can see; when in all actuality what you see is not what you get.

The spirit of man is the total man. When Lazarus died Jesus seemed somewhat callous about the whole ordeal in that he showed up way too late to heal Lazarus before he died. Then after he died, Jesus still waited a few days before he came out to see about his friend and his friend's family. It appeared as if Jesus really gave no energy to the death of his dear friend. He showed no concern. The reason why He did not show any urgency is that Jesus knew that his friend was not dead at all. His friend was only asleep.

Our friend Lazarus sleepeth; but I go, that I may awake him out of sleep. John 11:11

The important thing to see here, is that you must open your eyes. God is the maker of both your eyes and your ears. He made them for your benefit. But not knowing what the proper function and use of those organs are will cause them to become a curse to you instead of the blessing that they were originally intended to be. In the same manner though, sleep was intended to invigorate and replenish the exhausted soul. When given the proper amounts, sleep is an indescribable blessing. It can cause you to function at unusual levels of proficiency and alertness.

On the other end too much sleep quickly becomes anathematized, as onlookers condemn your laziness, knowing that such a person will find himself or herself drowning in the abyss of poverty and lack. Something that is fundamentally good can be turned inside out and become evil. Your eyes and your ears are both beneficial to you. However, if you persist in hearing the wrong things and observing bad sights, you will become the very thing that you observe. Open your eyes. Watch what you see.

Holocaust survivor Victor Emil Frankl refused to observe with his eyes the atrocities that were in fact happening right before him. He literally shut down his mental faculties so that they could not perceive things as others perceived them. Just imagine if Dr. Frankl fully observed the dead bodies, the stench of decaying flesh, and the sounds of earsplitting squeals from the tortured Jews in the concentration camps. What would Frankl's future have looked like? Quite obviously he too would have become a product of everything that he observed. He too would have been destroyed. Instead he chose in his mind to observe things that were totally different around him.

He chose to observe things that would fill his soul with fanciful hopes of surviving this onslaught and yet being able to tell his own story. When you close your eyes, you open your eyes to a totality new reality at the same time. And when you open your eyes you must be careful not to close off the options that life offers you each day. What are you observing with your eyes? Are you observing negative things around you? Are you observing lack, a recession, depressive states of mind, or terminal illness? If you are, then you will inevitably become the product of what you are viewing. You will become the form of whatever you incessantly observe.

DO YOU KNOW YOUR NAME?

If someone came up to you and asked you, "What is your name?" You would politely answer, "I am _____." You would respond with your birth name or surname. That's only the polite thing to do. But really, do you know your name? Do you know who you really are? Or have you simply been responding to the multiple names that you have been called all your life? One of the saddest things in life is to walk through life and not know who you are. Even your adversary knows who you are, although he will not willingly admit it. Do you remember the seven sons of Sceva?

Then certain of the vagabond Jews, exorcists, took upon them to call over them which had evil spirits the name of the Lord Jesus, saying, We adjure you by Jesus whom Paul preacheth. And there were seven sons of one Sceva, a Jew, and chief of the priests, which did so. And the evil spirit answered and said, Jesus I know, and Paul I know; but who are ye? And the man in whom the evil spirit was leaped on them, and overcame them, and prevailed against them, so

that they fled out of that house naked and wounded.
Acts 19:13–16

What is interesting here is that when the sons of Sceva and the Jewish priests tried to cast the evil spirits out of the people possessing them, the evil spirits began to speak. They said, (paraphrasing) "We know Paul and Jesus but who are you to use the authority of Jesus' name when you don't know Jesus?" The spirits called Jesus by his name and the Apostle Paul by his name. Because this spirit was not a spirit of truth it could not accurately call Jesus or Paul by their divine names. The evil spirit could only do that if it were able to perceive their divine nature.

So this evil spirit did not really know their rightful names. However, what the spirit did know is that both Jesus and Paul had authority to terminate his work. As far as the spirit was concerned, it really did not matter what their names were, he knew that they had authority to cast him out. The sons of Sceva and the chief priests did not have authority although they invoked the name of Jesus. In Christendom people have tried to force this scripture into a counterfeit interpretation hinting that these men who were experimenting in Jesus' Name must have had some kind of moral failure in their lives.

I've heard church folks use this scripture to condemn people who they thought were unworthy or not really anointed to perform such sacred functions. They'd say proudly, "Paul I know, Jesus I know but who are you?" They would take the scripture out of context trying to instill fear in people's minds. When in fact, the esoteric point here is that the seven sons of Sceva, and also the priests, did not know who they were. They didn't know their own name. They did not know their own identity. They had no idea what their destiny was. The person who does not have a strong sense of destiny will continually face cyclical conflicts.

When Jesus walked the earth, it did not matter as much for his sake who knew him. He needed to know who he was. That was far more important. Perhaps the most aggravating problem in society today is that most people do not know who they are. They are walking through life completely aimless, having no direction or sense of identity. Jesus was able to cast out evil spirits, as was Paul because they knew their true identity. Opposition will always overcome you when you don't know where you stand. Jesus knew who he was. Jesus said:

I and my Father are one. John 10:30

And,

Yet a little while, and the world seeth me no more; but ye see me: because I live, ye shall live also. At that day ye shall know that I am in my Father, and ye in me, and I in you. John 14:19–20

How is it possible to still see Jesus when no one else in the world can see Him? That is only possible when you know who you are—one with Christ. God knows you by your true name and nature. He does not call me by my given name, "Bernard." That name came to me when I entered into my earthly form. Long before that, before I was born on earth, I had a name, and God spoke to me regularly by that name. That is the name that He wants me to respond to when He calls. In order for that to happen for you or me the limits have got to go.

You have to take the limits off and begin to understand that you are just a great big ball of energy trapped in matter. The key is not to become trapped in this arena. You may be mentally trapped on the porch trying to get in to the house. You'll stay there as long as you continue to embrace self-imposed limitations, or the limitations that you allowed others to place on you. God has prepared a place for you. That place is not necessarily a physical or geographical location as much as it is a place of consciousness. This place of consciousness is where you are supposed to be.

*In my Father's house are many mansions : if it were not so, I would have told you. I go to prepare a place for you. And if I go and prepare a place **(in your consciousness)** for you, I will come again, and receive you unto myself; that where I am, there ye may be also. John 14:2–3 (bold is author's own)*

When you understand in consciousness that the place you are supposed to be is a wealthy place, impoverished surroundings will never be an option for you again. But in order to shed poverty and the feeling of being deprived and second-rated, you must first understand how you came to think the way that you do. Everything in our society has a direct impact on the way you think and feel. In fact, I would say that society teaches you how to feel and think about nearly everything, including God. Retail companies pay out billions of dollars annually to get people to purchase their goods by using great marketing tactics.

You see their advertising campaigns on billboards everywhere, where merchants are marketing their wares. In the same way, the oppressor has done a remarkable job of marketing the way you should feel and think about who you are. They have even gone as far as to tell you who you are. They named you. They told you what God to serve, how to serve Him, and what He would look like. They plastered images all across the walls and stained glass windows of cathedrals and said, "This is the image of God, serve ye Him."

Anything that did not look similar to the image of God that they prescribed for you was an imposter, and an evil person. What difference does all of this make? This makes all the difference in the world. These images became the basis for your daily meditation and you have meditated on them so long, that it is rather difficult to erase those images that have been indelibly branded on your mind. You have accepted all of these images as truth. Anyone who dares to challenge the veracity of the images that they have set up for you will be ridiculed, condemned to hell. Such manipulation of the mind is nothing less than cruelty.

No one has the right to manipulate thought seeking to subvert the mind and all that it has come to believe as true. Clinical Psychologist and professor of African psychology at Florida State

University, Dr. Naim Akbar in his groundbreaking book, *Chains and Images of Psychological Slavery* comments on this mental subversion:

As cruel and painful as chattel slavery was, it could be exceeded only by a worse form of slavery.

The slavery that captures the mind and incarcerates the motivation, perception, aspiration, and identity in a web of anti-self images, generating a personal and collective self-destruction, is more cruel than the shackles on the wrists and ankles. The slavery that feeds on the psychology, invading the soul of man, destroying his loyalties to himself and establishing allegiance to forces which destroy him, is an even worse form of capture. Pg 2

Students of the mind have not adequately dealt with the influence of religious symbols and imagery on thinking people. Perhaps the Swiss Psychologist, Carl Jung, is a distinct exception to this statement, for he has discussed in considerable detail the importance of symbols in general, and religious symbols in particular, on the thinking of human beings. He argues for their relevance to psychological and mental health, and also identifies the impact of their absence or distorted occurrence. Jung does not (nor does any other psychologist) discuss the specific impact of these images, or any religious imagery on the psyches of African people. It is important to keep in mind that the images of God which a people have will determine the expanses of their mind. Pgs 38–39

Dr. Akbar challenges us to think about the correlation between the image of God and the vastness of your mind's ability to create, to own, or to control as God controls. If you believe that you are inferior to anyone then that will be evident in your thoughts, as the fruit of those inferior thoughts will always equate to reckless behavior. This is no excuse for the irresponsible actions of a people. It only gives a valid reason why such actions may exist. When you give a people a limited selection of mental images from which to choose, you limit them severely.

The best decision for all people is to not wait for anyone to give you the selection but rather create your own selection and then choose from the smorgasbord of the feast before you. You will take on the form of what you mediate on. So, you must be very careful. Far too many people have taken on the form of another god, a god other than God Himself, a god other than the God within. Adopting this false identity has caused millions of innocent seekers to take on the form of the one who oppresses them, condemning them to an eternity of bondages.

You must break free from the psychological chains that have held you back from seizing your prize in life. Until now you have only done what you were forced to do or given permission to do. To break out of this repressive modality you must begin to choose a new identity and renounce the former one that your oppressor gave to you. You must choose to be God, for beside Him there is no other.

••• MEDITATIVE THOUGHT •••

You must break free from the psychological chains that have held you back from seizing your prize in life.

UNFORMED PURPOSES

And God saw the light, that it was good: and God divided the light from the darkness. Genesis 1:4

I feel it would be safe to conclude that God's original state was darkness. God had to divide the light from the darkness for however long a period of time, then one day He simply said, "Let Me be light." God was sitting in the dark for a long time until He spoke light into the darkness. Like God, you have been sitting in the same darkness waiting to give form.

Jesus is known as the first-born among *many* brethren. You are the many brethren and you are getting ready to be born. You will walk as sons and daughters of God. Only sons can understand the mystery of the Godhead. If you are a son, you must be a son of something. Whatever you behold, you become the son of that which you are beholding. Only when you behold the Father do you become a Son of God born from God. You are the original authentic S.O.B. (son of beholding).

Don't despise what you behold whether it is good or bad. In all reality it's all good, and it's all

God. What I mean is that even the so-called bad things that you behold still give credence to your life's mission. You need misery in order to have a legitimate ministry. Out of your misery your ministry is birthed. You need a mess in order to get a message. In order for you to see the hand of God revealed to you like never before, you are going to have a complex situation appear in your life.

If you have never lived through a season when it didn't seem as if God was there then you still have more forming that needs to take place in your life. Infants cry and holler when they are not comforted every minute. You have to change their diapers, feed them, or rock them to sleep. That is what they need, and that is also what keeps them babies. They need to have the assurance that someone is always close by. They are completely helpless.

As a maturing believer, your growth is not determined by how well you perform when divinity walks with you throughout each moment in life. No, not at all, your growth is determined by your ability to keep walking forward through the valley of the shadows of death and not knowing exactly whether or not God is even nearby. The hell and misery that you are going through or that you've already graduated from is just a signal that you are at the dawning of a brand new day. My encouragement to you is to hang in there; God is bound to separate the light from the darkness.

WITHOUT FORM

And the earth was without form, and void; and darkness was upon the face of the deep. And the Spirit of God moved upon the face of the waters. Genesis 1:2

I beheld the earth, and, lo, it was without form, and void; and the heavens, and they had no light. Jeremiah 4:23

Meditation has everything to do with the idea of "without form." Without form has everything to do with the whole notion of creation. Anytime God or the God in you creates anything, that creation always begins without form; it is void, and it is surrounded by darkness. Everything that is or ever will become begins with a thought. It begins in the mind. Once the thought has been established, that is when it is ready to take on a form and evolve from its barren state to bear fruit. The inside of your mind is a great example of what darkness looks like.

You could never dissect a thought unless you went in a totally dark room to discover what it actually consists of. This is why the ministry of the prophet is much needed in a world full of darkness. The prophet whose words are analogous to the earth in its inception bares a striking resemblance, in that the word begins without any form. It is in its innate state, completely void. It is only a word, so the fruit to be born from it does not yet exist on the material plane.

For both the prophet and the receiver the word is surrounded by darkness; particularly since the word of hope bears no similarity to their present state of affairs. Somewhere within, you must know that the word of the Lord is not only germane to your needs, but that it must be imagined into being through constant meditation. That is why the prophets will tell people to meditate on your word, pray on your word, and quote the word that you've received on a regular basis. By speaking forth the word you are literally giving the thing, which has no form, tangibility.

CHAPTER EIGHT

Putting Your Meditation Into Practice

You have successfully reached the final chapter of this book and the first chapter of your new lifestyle of meditation. Congratulations! Up until this point you have been given a very solid foundation on which to base all of your meditative pursuits. You know what meditation is and how it works. Now I want to show you how to put everything that you have learned into practice. I want to show you how to meditate and apply it to your life to get results. While there are various ways to meditate, and no one way is superior over the other, I will share with you the practice that many mystics have successfully used that has proven to be beneficial to them and also me.

For your convenience, I have listed *five practical steps* to entering into your personal zone. Know this; these are not ironclad rules. They are suggested guidelines. Each person will customize these guiding principles to best fit their personality and the personal objectives that they are reaching for. Meditation is not a "once in a while" impulse that you act on sporadically. Meditation is a lifestyle that is formed through daily habits. Jesus meditated every day of his life, which is perhaps one of the ways that he stayed so mentally focused and inwardly balanced.

You will not master these principles on your first day or even in the first month that you initiate this way of life. It will take years before you truly master the art of meditation. Be of good cheer! Unlike other disciplines of the spirit, meditation is one where you receive peaceful exchange as your reward early on. You don't have to be a master to encounter the rewards. They will come quickly. Because of that quick return (which usually comes first in the form of an overwhelming sense of peace), you will be self-motivated from that point on to press on further, believing for even better incentives on the course of your exciting journey. Now let's begin.

FIVE PRACTICAL STEPS

1. Learn how to enter into the silence. *Be still, and know that I am God: I will be exalted among the heathen, I will be exalted in the earth. Psalms 46:10*

Prayer in its most genuine sense is meditation. And meditation is prayer. The difficult thing for most believers to understand is how prayer can be connected with silence, when most people think of prayer as an auditory dialogue between God and His family. The most effective prayer is mediation. The Apostle Paul readily admits that Christians generally do not know what to pray for when using their carnal minds.

Likewise the Spirit also helpeth our infirmities: for we know not what we should pray for as we ought: but the Spirit itself maketh intercession for us with groanings which cannot be uttered. Romans 8:26

It is when we enter into the silence that we participate in high Holy Communion with our Lord. This is meditation. Here we discover not what we want God to hear from us, but rather what He desires to reveal to us. Revelation comes through meditation. It comes in the silence. God would never shout over the boisterous noise and thunderous clamor of our busy lives. God will never allow Himself to enter into such a competition for He is God. When it is time for His voice to be heard, it is perceived quietly through ardently listening ears eager to hear God's still small voice. You must quiet your mind.

> ••• MEDITATIVE THOUGHT •••
>
> *The most effective prayer is mediation.*

Turn off the television. Cut off your favorite music. Above and beyond that, turn off the noise that reverberates within you, and just hear and listen. That's all. Don't expect too much at this stage. This step is all about getting you to appreciate the discipline of an inner sanctity of silence. It is understandable that if you were not taught this from early on, that it might be a bit awkward at first. But in time you will not only appreciate the silence, but will find that your life will not be able to progress forward even one step until you have begun your day by entering in.

Episcopal priest, Morton T. Kelsey wrote *The Other Side of Silence: A Guide to Christian Meditation*, which was one of the first ground-breaking books on the topic of meditation ever written to the modern church. In it he uncovers the conventional thought of most Christians when it comes to silence and why. He also details how and why Eastern religions commonly accept silence with much greater regard than do Christians. He writes:

The idea of linking silence with prayer may sound like an out-and-out contradiction to many Christians. We are accustomed to thinking of the familiar forms of prayer that people use when they join together to worship or ask God for something. These forms almost always follow a lead given in the past.

There is another, equally important way of praying in which a person becomes silent and tries to listen instead of speaking. Instead of picking up a familiar lead and speaking about the things that all of us feel are needed, one tries to become still. One effort is to be silent enough to hear, first, the deepest needs of one's own heart, and then the prompting of the creative Spirit in whatever direction it may indicate. In the second kind of prayer, which we call meditation, one is trying to follow one's inner road as it is opened. (pg 93)

Of Eastern Religions Kelsey observed these things:

No one in Eastern religions doubts the value of silence. The practice of being alone in stillness is certainly central in Hindu religion. Yoga and also various forms of Buddhist meditation begin and end in silence. Throughout Zen the value of utter stillness is emphasized; the goal of satori is to reach this ultimate peace, and the novice begins searching while sitting still in the lotus position. There is a strong tradition in Chinese religious thought that the way of coming into harmony with the tao, which is the ultimate principle of reality, is by inner quiet, by stilling the inner confusion so that one comes to peace and harmony within. Almost the same approach is found in certain sects of Islamic religion. (pg 94)

Obviously many Eastern Religions are far more at peace with peace than most Christians are. This is a very serious concern especially since meditation is one of the most necessary missing components of the Christian's experience that has been absent for far too long. So learn to make it a habit of spending time in silence each day of your life. Try to make it the same time each time, as to build a consistent habit. It may be for only three, five or ten minutes. The length of your silence is not as important as the quality of your silence.

2. Grasp an image of the thing that you desire. You have to have a concrete image of what your focus is. Remember that whatever you behold you become. So in order to get the best results from meditating you have to have an image always before you in your mind. Sometimes I meditate just to clear my mind. When that is my objective I have an intangible image before me. I may imagine being surrounded by the most peaceful atmosphere I have ever been in. Peace and oneness with God is my focus. And as long as I hold that image in my mind then I will become that. The things that you take hold of can be material or immaterial. The principle works regardless of what kind of thing it is. So you must have an object of desire. Again, the object may be tangible or ethereal.

3. Understand that visualization brings about materialization. You must practice the art of visualizing the thing that you desire. You have an object of your desire before you, but now you must take the next step and begin to visualize what you see to the point that you actually start to feel like you what you are beholding. This is not a trick on words, this is very literal. And for anyone who has entered into this area of visualization, they would agree that anything that they have ever visualized, their desires only manifested after they sensed a strong feeling associated with the thing desired. This is a powerful aspect of entering in. You will begin to feel like the thing that you desire. You will feel like the car, you will feel like the promotion, you will feel like the new home. Your feeling will guide you safely to your desired destination. You will feel yourself there. No one ever receives anything in life until they first feel it.

••• MEDITATIVE THOUGHT •••

You only buy things with your mind.

Early on in my ministry when my young parishioners would desire new cars, I would tell them to go to the car dealership and first test-drive the car. They needed to get a feeling of how they would actually look and feel while driving the car of their dreams. Sometimes I would get a bit of resistance, "Bishop I don't have the money to buy that car." I would let them know that the money is really not the issue, the issue is visualizing yourself in the car and feeling as if it is so. The majority of the people who went to the dealerships didn't have the manifested budget to purchase an expensive bicycle at the time, let alone a brand new automobile. As sure as day, nearly all of them bought the car that they went to test drive. Why is this? The reason why they were able to get the car, and circumvent the standardized process is they came to realize that you do not buy anything in life with money.

You only buy things with your mind. Another point worth sharing is that I would also tell them on the first visit to make sure that they get a few brochures of the exact car that they wanted. Tear out the pages and paste them or tape them in the top three areas where you will spend the most time viewing. For some, that place was the mirror in the bathroom as they shaved or put on makeup. Some people put the picture in the window of their car. Some put the picture above their stove in the kitchen so they could visualize it as they prepared dinner for the family. Others placed the picture in the corner of their computer screen since they sat at their desk looking at the screen all day. I wanted them to visualize the thing that would eventually become them.

Shakti Gawain in her seminal work *Creative Visualization: Using The Power of Your Imagination To Create What You Want In Your Life* says: *Imagination is the ability to create an idea, a mental picture, or a feeling sense of something. In creative visualization you use your imagination to create a clear image, idea, or feeling of something you wish to manifest. Then you continue to focus on the idea, feeling, or picture regularly, giving it positive energy until it becomes objective reality... in other words, until you actually achieve what you have been imagining. Your goal may be on any level— physical, emotional, mental, or spiritual. (pg 4)*

A word of caution is that you must not get too locked into the phrasing visualization and allow that to limit you from entering into the experience based on what you may have heard others express about their own personal experiences. Remember every person is different and each experience will be very different from one person to the next. Don't get stuck whether you see images very clearly or rather you just feel a strong inward feeling about something that you desire. Both are green lights that you may move ahead safely. Gawain says,

Don't get stuck on the term "visualize." It is not at all necessary to mentally see an image. Some people say they see very clear, sharp images when they close their eyes and imagine

something. Others don't really "see" anything; they sense or feel it, or they just sort of "think about" it. That's perfectly fine. Some people are more visually oriented, some more auditory, others are more kinesthetic. We all use our imaginations constantly—it's impossible not to, so whatever process you find yourself doing when you imagine in fine. (pg 19)

One of the things that seekers are taught to say is, "I AM that." There is no other power in the earth other than the power of I AM. And whatever you attach to I AM gives that thing the power to be. It gives it the power to become yours. You may say I AM healing. I AM salvation. I AM peace. I AM joy. I AM debt free. I AM increase, and so on. Whatever the thing that you visualize, be sure to make daily confessions that I AM that thing, and you will become the thing that you desire.

4. Meditate with the end in mind. This is sometimes a difficult area to understand since so many people focus more on their beginning or the draining process of becoming what they envision. You have to see yourself at the end, place the thought of the fulfillment of being there and then begin to meditate on that end result. You don't have to worry about starting from the beginning. Your physical body will travel from the beginning to the end. What you visualize, you see it as an end. You then travel to that place in consciousness, and then your body will back up to the beginning, your starting point, and then allow you to begin journeying toward that thing you see. Why is this? Why don't you just stay physically there, at the place where your mind is beholding? Your body will always have to catch up to the place that you are in consciousness. You see, your body is bound by nearly every earthly restriction. Your mind is not. Your mind can travel outside of your body at will. No need to make any prior reservations or worry about whether or not your travel plans will be overcrowded with other fellow travelers.

You can travel anywhere, at anytime, for any reason that you so choose. There are no constraints. As they say the sky is the limit. I disagree. The sky is not the limit. There are no limits unless you conjure limitations up in your mind. The Apostle Paul had such an experience where his physical body could not hold him back from his travel plans, the ones previously booked by his consciousness. There were many things that he did not fully comprehend on this trip. But the greater thing to understand here is that he went to this place in his mind, and it became of living reality to him. You can never travel to anyplace in this world or in the outer world that you have not first traveled to in your mind.

It is not expedient for me doubtless to glory. I will come to visions and revelations of the Lord. I knew a man in Christ above fourteen years ago, (whether in the body, I cannot tell; or whether out of the body, I cannot tell: God knoweth;) such an one caught up to the third heaven. And I knew such a man, (whether in the body, or out of the body, I cannot tell: God knoweth; How that he was caught up into paradise, and heard unspeakable words, which it is not lawful for a man to utter. Of such an one will I glory: yet of myself I will not glory, but in mine infirmities.
2 Corinthians 12:1–5

New York Times Best-Selling Author and Leadership expert Stephen Covey shares in his book, *The 7 Habits of Highly Effective People: Powerful Lessons in Personal Change* one of the seven habits, being Habit 2: Begin with the End in Mind.

Although Habit 2 applies to many different circumstances and levels of life, the most fundamental application of "begin with the end in mind" is to begin today with the image, picture, or paradigm of the end of your life as your frame of reference or the criterion by which everything is examined. Each part of your life—today's behavior, tomorrow's behavior, next week's behavior, next month's behavior—can be examined in the context of the whole, of what really matters most to you. By keeping that end clearly in mind, you can make certain that whatever you do on any particular day does not violate the criteria you have defined as supremely important, and that each day of your life contributes in a meaningful way to the vision you have of your life as a whole. To begin with the end in mind means to start with a clear understanding of your destination. It means to know where you're going so that you better understand where you are now and so that the steps you tale are always in the right direction.

Begin with the end in mind!

5. Understand that meditating is contemplating you out. Why is God so mindful of you? Look at the word contemplate. It means to look at or think about intently. When a person contemplates something they have the thing in mind as a possibility. They make plans concerning the things with which they are contemplating. So then, God is contemplating you out from your beginning to end. God thinks about you and has already made dinner plans for you and Him to feast together. The reason why He has you on His mind is because He knows that He can become you and experience life in the earth realm through you. That is why he is so mindful of you. David spoke of God's fascination over you in Psalms:

What is man, that thou art mindful of him? and the son of man, that thou visitest him? For

thou hast made him a little lower than the angels,
and hast crowned him with glory and honour.
Thou madest him to have dominion over the
works of thy hands; thou hast put all things
under his feet: Psalms 8:4–6

••• MEDITATIVE THOUGHT •••

Complaining is meditation in reverse.
When you complain you are essentially
allowing the problem to become
larger than the answer.

Succinctly put, God is meditating on you all of the time. Again, this principle works both ways. You become what you behold. Whatever you meditate on you will become. God becomes you and I since He spends so much time creating a template in you so that He can dwell within it. That is what contemplation is all about. That works for you the same way. What you meditate upon, you are actually contemplating, or in other words you are making a template for what you continually focus on. If you change your focus then you will recreate your template. If you want change in your life, then destroy your old template and create a new one through new focus seasoned with a vast imagination, and you will begin to see new things happen in your life. The most accurate example of how God contemplated Himself is found in John.

In the beginning was the Word, and the Word was with God, and the Word was God. The same was in the beginning with God. All things were made by him; and without him was not any thing made that was made. In him was life; and the life was the light of men. And the light shineth in darkness; and the darkness comprehended it not. John 1:1–5

Change your contemplations and change your life!

As we begin to wind this lesson down, I would like you to be aware of just a few things that are very important to your understanding of mediation. First, beware of complaining. Don't do it at all. Complaining is the sin that prevented the children of Israel from *entering into* the Promised Land. In the same manner, complaining will prohibit you from *entering into* your Promised Land. Complaining is meditation in reverse. When you complain you are essentially allowing the problem to become larger than the answer. You literally set up a template for it to manifest. Give no place for murmuring and complaining.

••• MEDITATIVE THOUGHT •••

Remember that concentrated "feeling" hardens any imagination into a fact.

The cure for the murmuring and complaining seems rather obvious. But I shall enlighten you nonetheless. There is nothing on earth that can top the spirit of gratitude, praise and thanksgiving. Having a grateful spirit is one of the surest ways to get "more" in your life. Be thankful for what you have. Never complain about that which you do not have, for in doing so you confuse the all of creation who knows well that everything that you need has already been installed on the inside of you. Get full of fulfillment. Get full of what you are feeling. Remember that concentrated "feeling" hardens any imagination into a fact. Everything in life starts in thought. You cannot even meditate without a thought. All that you have ever dreamed and hoped for is only a meditation away!

About The Author

Bishop E. Bernard Jordan is nothing less than a modern day prophet. In 1989 he predicted the 2005 Gulf Coast natural disaster, storm Katrina that had a devastating effect on the people in New Orleans. Sought after by nations of the world for his accurate prophecies, Jordan has prophesied the word of the Lord to literally millions of people. He is noted for his uncanny accuracy of the prophecies that he ministers. Businessmen, political officials, celebrities and churches are numbered among the thousands who have consulted Bishop Jordan for counsel and direction through the Word of the Lord.

The Master Prophet has traveled to Swaziland, South Africa, and delivered the Word of the Lord to the Queen and the Royal Family. He has prophesied in many nations, including Germany, Canada, Korea and the Caribbean, bringing an astute word of counsel to the leadership and royalty of those countries. In February 1988, he was invited to address a special assembly of ambassadors and diplomats at the United Nations concerning the oppressive racism in South Africa. He addressed the assembly again in February 1992, and prophesied of the impending liberation of South Africa, which has come to pass.

He has been featured on NBC's *Today Show*, FOX 5, *Good Day New York*, CNN, and many, many others. He was also featured in *The Daily News*, *New York Times*, *New York Post* and *Newsday* with some of his congregates as well as in an interview in *Billboard Magazine* on his views concerning social issues. His life-changing messages on reformation and liberation have sparked acclaim, as well as controversy, as he teaches the unadulterated Word of God. He is the founder of Zoë Ministries in New York City, a prophetic gathering with a vision to impact the globe with Christ's message of liberation.

Bishop Jordan has written more than 40 books including best-sellers, *Mentoring*, *Spiritual Protocol*, *What Every Woman Should Know About Men*, *The Power of Money*, *and Cosmic*

Economics, and *New York Times* Bestseller, *The Laws of Thinking: 20 Secrets to Using The Divine Power of Your Mind To Manifest Prosperity*. He holds his Doctorate in Religious Studies and a Ph.D. in Religious Studies. He and his wife Pastor Debra have five children. You can watch him live on television on The Power of Prophecy telecast or through live streaming, just visit his site at www.bishopjordan.com.

For Further Reading
by Bishop E. Bernard Jordan:

The Business of Getting Rich: 12 Secrets to Unveiling The Spiritual Side of Wealth In You

Cosmic Economics: The Universal Keys To Wealth

Dreams & Visions: Letters from God and How To Read Them!

Prophetic Congress: Deep Calleth Unto Deep

Prophetic Congress: The Summit Volume II

Prophetic Genesis

School of the Prophets Volume I

School of the Prophets Volume II

Spiritual Protocol

Unveiling The Mysteries

The Laws of Thinking: 20 Secrets to Using the Divine Power of Your Mind to Manifest Prosperity

The Marital Union of Thought

The Science of Prophecy

From Pastor Debra A. Jordan:

Prophetic Reflections: Poetry From the Heart of the Prophetess

FREE
WRITTEN
PROPHECY

As seen on TV!

To get your free personal written word
in the mail from me,
Master Prophet E. Bernard Jordan,
simply visit our site at
www.bishopjordan.com
and follow the prompts.

The Master Prophet will see the Mind of God
on your behalf and he will give you the
ANSWERS YOU HAVE BEEN SEEKING.

Notes

Notes

Notes

Notes

Notes